May the Rivers Never Sleep

Bill & John McMillan

May the Rivers Never Sleep

Bill & John McMillan

Frank Amato
Publications
Portland

All inquiries should be addressed to:
Frank Amato Publications, Inc. • P.O. Box 82112 • Portland, Oregon 97282
503-653-8108 • www.AmatoBooks.com

Photography by Bill McMillan & John R. McMillan unless otherwise noted
Illustration by John McMillan

ISBN-10: 1-57188-480-7
ISBN-13: 978-1-57188-480-0
UPC: 0-81127-00322-8

Printed in Singapore

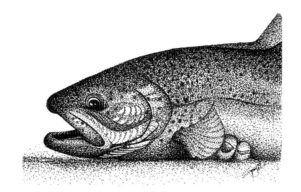

Table of Contents

Foreword 11

Introduction: Rivers of Revelation 12

January: When the Steelhead Now Enter 24

February: The Water Ouzel's Song 35

March: Climatic Tantrums and Gladiators 42

April: Rivers Determined by Waterfalls 50

May: Guards and Sneakers 58

June: A Solstice Song to Trout 68

July: Canyon Steelhead and Headwater Trout 79

August: Evolving Char and Increasing Pink Salmon 88

September: Time of Transition and Movement 98

October: The Ice Travelers and Renewal of Vision 108

November: Death and Deserts 116

December: Flood, Ice, Snow and Salmon and Steelhead at Glacier Toes 129

A River Calendar's Future 138

North Fork Salmonberry River, Oregon in April 1995.

Roderick Haig-Brown, 1972.

Dedicated to:

The conservation legacy of Roderick Haig-Brown
and to all those women and men who follow in
the vision of his footsteps in the protection and
recovery of wild fish and wild ecosystems.

So long as man marked his life only by the cycles of nature — the changing seasons, the waxing and waning moon — he remained a prisoner of nature. If he was to go his own way and fill his world with human novelties, he would have to make his own measure of time.

—Daniel J. Boorstin,
The Discoverers (1983)

Snake River Washington

Chronology of Differing Human Measures of Time

20,000-35,000 years ago 28-29-day moon cycles carved on bones and antlers

18,000 years ago 28-29-day moon cycles depicted in animal art in caves of France

10,000-15,000 years ago native Americans led by moon and natural food cycles

9,000-11,000 years ago early agriculture led by Yangtze/Yellow river flood cycles and the moon

6,760 years ago Assyrian lunar calendar begins; new year begins with spring

6,250 years ago more complex Egyptian 365-day solar calendar begins; new year begins with annual Nile flood

5,025-3,370 years ago Olmec/Mayan calendar begins; the oldest had complexly determined 260-day year

2,056 years ago Julius Caesar's visit to Egypt results in 365-day Julian solar calendar; new year begins January 1st

429 years ago, Pope Gregory XIII commissions the mathematically complex Gregorian calendar of 365.2425 days with a 366-day leap year every four years

65 years ago, publication of *A River Never Sleeps* with time measured by cyclic life in rivers

Foreword

As long as I live I'll hear waterfalls and birds and winds sing. I'll interpret the rocks, learn the language of flood, storm, and avalanche. I'll acquaint myself with the glaciers and wild gardens and get as near the heart of the world as I can.

John Muir, America's first conservationist stated these words in his book *My First Summer in the Sierra*. These words are quite profound and succinctly explain the essence of the book you are about to read - *May the Rivers Never Sleep*. Bill and John McMillan share a view of rivers, salmon, steelhead, and the Pacific Northwest, with Muir, that is based on the mantra that diverse languages of nature offer endless opportunity for interpretation and revelation. Their experiences on Pacific Northwest rivers are conveyed through the filters of history, angling, snorkeling, photography, observation, and contemplation. Each is tied together through the ultimate filters of time and space: the seasonal changes that rivers undergo over the course of the year. The book is not only their perspective though, but also that of previous McMillan generations and of other anglers, naturalists, and scientists whose observations have provided context, knowledge, and ultimately understanding.

The essence of the book is the physical and biological tapestry of river time, a concept fostered by Roderick Haig-Brown, the father of salmon conservation in the Pacific Northwest. His ideas, writings, and actions were the stimulus for Bill and John's writings and photographs. As a consequence, this book pays homage to their favorite Haig-Brown book: *A River Never Sleeps*. The father and son have found a common bond in rivers. This bond, which is ultimately equally tied to Bill's father and Haig-Brown, is clearly reflected in their writing and photography. I know of few – if any – other people so enamored with the life and history of rivers and salmon. Bill and John have spent thousands of hours using all the filters to view rivers. I find that each month in this book offers a blend of experiences, some of which we have all likely shared, and rarer ones too, those experienced only by people who call the rivers their lifeblood.

I am a father, husband, son, conservationist, and scientist who has been blessed in hearing many of these stories and observations during my 17 years of friendship with Bill and John. We have shared many of our lives' experiences and lessons during that time. Not everyone has been privy to these experiences. Many of those stories and observations are herein described through the mediums of writing and photography rather than conversation. Enjoy the stories, admire the photos, and appreciate the diverse filters employed by Bill and John to more closely understand the ecosystems of our Pacific Northwest rivers. I too, like Bill and John, believe that the rivers are truly our lifeblood. Being close to rivers – their movement of water coursing across the landscape – is as close as one can get to the heart of nature: may they never sleep.

George Pess ~ geomorphologist, fisheries biologist,
and frequent field companion of the McMillan Clan

Introduction

Rivers of Revelation

Roderick Haig-Brown's neighbor and friend, Van Egan,
wades the Campbell River in August of 1986.

I once came upon an anecdote about a Chinese sage waiting for a ferry en route to his hermitage in the mountains. As he waited he happened on an old fisherman along the riverbank. The fisherman repetitively cast out his line with skill, but there was no hook. Mystified, the sage asked:

"Dear fisherman, I have noticed that you fish without a hook. How, may I ask, do you intend to catch a fish?"

The old fisherman replied, "Kind sage, my purpose is not to catch a fish."

Our canoe camp half-way between Megin Lake and Shelter Inlet in 1983.

Rivers are among those places where revelations can occur, but we can be so focused by narrow intent of purpose it obscures our ability to experience that larger vision. I once thought this was the fault of the Calvinist pox on the American psyche in my rebellion to our educational system in the 1960s – educations to provide cogs in the Western corporate wheel, rather than the larger Eastern wheel of Tao. There has since come an inkling both wheels miss the point of human opportunity and human responsibility in the lives we represent in the here and now.

In that early rebellion to the Calvinist pox, I came to fall back on the example of lives outside the perceived contagion – whether Western or Eastern. One of these was Henry Thoreau, oft quoted in his plea for lives of simplicity, but seldom used as an example to actually emulate in the panic that, God forbid, where would corporate employees come from if young people chose lives as hermits in the woods?

The other was that of the Canadian, Roderick Haig-Brown, comparatively little known outside the interests of fly fishermen, but whose work some critics include among the best nature writing of the mid 20th century. In 1926, at the age of 18 and disillusioned by his negative experience of what English education provided, he was faced with the immediate choices of Oxford, or military or civil service in the Colonial Empire as described by his daughter Valerie in *Deep Currents* (1997). Instead, he chose a freer vision for himself on the West Coast of North

Megin Shelter at Megin Lake in 1983.

America – first in a logging camp in Washington near the Stillaguamish River and then a more remote camp on Vancouver Island's Nimpkish River.

He briefly returned to England in 1929 at age 22, remaining long enough to write his first book, *Silver, the Life Story of an Atlantic Salmon*. Encouraged he might modestly support himself as a writer on nature, but would only disappoint his family's expectations in England, he gladly returned to the forests and rivers of Vancouver Island in 1931 where he decided he belonged. A writer he became, reared a family on Vancouver Island's Campbell River, and accepted the legal duties of a country magistrate in a community at the frontier edge. Despite common monetary struggles he fulfilled his vision of belonging to something he believed in beyond aristocratic comfort. His stubborn integrity would not yield to a life that was less.

I began reading Haig-Brown in junior high with publication of *Fisherman's Summer* in 1959. Continued reading of his books instilled a desire for belonging to forests and rivers as portrayed in his writings – particularly after reading *A River Never Sleeps*. Published in 1946, its essays describe his childhood, youth and early manhood of coming to find rivers as places of perpetual revelation through every season. I read it over and over, each time finding some passage that provided new inspiration.

Misty river morning on Westside Vancouver Island.

My own life on rivers began with a tiny fruit-picker's cabin rented on the Yakima River in 1968. In drives to and from college through the golden autumn light of the Kittitas Valley, or reading a book beside the silver ribbon of the Yakima, I little understood why anyone in their right mind would choose a dormitory or fraternity.

Two years later, I upgraded to a four-room cabin on the Washougal River just prior to marriage. Gradually remodeled to include two children, its river view was never twice the same: bright blue over anchor ice in January; brown with a bottom of rumbling boulders in December flood; emerald green in May with yellow and red ornaments of Western Tanagers decorating the maple tree outside my upper story writing window.

On divorce 19 years later, I retreated to seven years of solitude – first to a long abandoned cabin on the upper Washougal with a view to the river through draping hemlock and cedar boughs; then as caretaker of a little-used fishing lodge on Oregon's Grande Ronde River beneath a cathedral of basalt cliffs 2,000 feet high.

Today my wife and I live in a small, Depression-era farmhouse beside the jade flow of the Skagit River. We may end our days here, depending on which turns "dust to dust" first – us or the house.

It was not until nearly 40 years old that I came to more carefully reread the Haig-Brown books and to realize the transition he made from a fisherman to that of observer, naturalist, and conservationist in his last 25 years. About ten years later, I came across the anecdote of the Chinese fisherman as an Eastern spiritual parallel to Haig-Brown's more earth-based Western transition. Rivers are places of perpetual change – both natural and human caused. This is part of both their nature and their attraction provided by the ceaseless flow of water from mountains to the sea. But change can also present difficult adjustments.

In 1950's *Measure of the Year*, a 42-year-old Haig-Brown wrote with his early characteristic optimism regarding the consequences of two upper Campbell River dams above Elk Falls and how the altered flows may affect the salmon, his family, and his community downstream. Nine years later, in *Fisherman's Summer* it became evident after yet a third dam was built in the upper Campbell drainage that his native optimism had worn thin. Nevertheless, an inherent English stiff upper lip managed a tenuous thread of hope:

"The new conditions…open up a whole new field of exploration and the days are once again more lively and good."

Through persistence and invention he had discovered a few interesting fishing opportunities in lower Campbell River despite the radically altered watershed and subsequent summer torrent of a river harnessed to power production. This was juxtaposed to staggering losses of inundated forests, creeks, rivers, and lakes and related fish and wildlife in the upper Campbell country he never returned to again.

As a consequence of continuing loss, *Fisherman's Fall* of 1964 is perhaps Haig-Brown's most important book for the example of his adjustments and accepted responsibility to an altered Campbell River that can only now be evaluated as those of a visionary. They are now methods of modern science for revelations into the aquatic life of rivers. His altered outlook is evidenced in his conclusion about the rivers of North America:

"I am afraid for the future, as I suppose every thinking person must be. Yet even on this dark and sodden late October day I can feel hope and find assurance that something will be left long years from now of all I have seen and known."

Countering these concerns, in July of 1963 at age 55, Haig-Brown was introduced to snorkeling by a friend. While the Chinese fisherman bewildered the sage by fishing without a hook,

Revelation without a hook: Icicle Creek redband trout,
Wenatchee basin, during Wild Fish Conservancy research.

Haig-Brown became the Western equivalent by throwing away hook, line, rod and all for the freedom of unencumbrance:

"...I found myself immediately transported from the world of air to the world of water and at least as comfortable in the new world ...to my delight ...a place full of life and beauty.

It is a quiet sort of pastime, much like wandering through some strange, beautiful and unending garden where the fish seem exotic creatures miraculously and perfectly naturalized, ideally matched to place and setting...everything is as it must and should be, yet everything is also new and breath-taking experience, a wonder of seeing that never stales.

I wondered...if there may not be times...when the rod...is an encumbrance, a responsibility that interferes with the simpler and keener pleasures of seeing and hearing and feeling and finding...the eyes and mind are free to turn attention to the whole scene instead of concentrating on some small fraction of it."

In April of 1983, Don Collis of Sooke, B.C. and Jim Abbott of Victoria invited me to join them to explore the largest remaining unlogged watershed on Vancouver Island. The Megin River flows south from Splendor Mountain in Strathcona Park, and then into and out of Megin Lake. Indeed, the noun "splendor" is the appropriate word, no mere adjective, for the river, the lake, and mountain backdrop.

The Megin River proved to be a turning point in my life. My previous interest in rivers had almost entirely focused on fishing – particularly fly fishing, and particularly fly fishing for steelhead. Thereafter, it increasingly became revelation without a hook.

John on Washougal River at age five.

Don and Jim had worked in remote logging camps in their youth where stories were told of an old, moss-covered shelter tucked away in ancient forest along the shores of Megin Lake. It was said to have a logbook containing the names of those few souls who managed to reach its remote location. Seven miles inland from Shelter Inlet, isolated in a valley of immense spruce and cedar, the Megin Log had become something of a legend among British Columbia outdoorsmen. They hoped to find the Megin Log, examine the art work and inspired writings it was said to contain, add their names to those who had reached the shelter, and provide a note of how we had arrived...the old way...the Canadian way. That would be *upstream* travel by canoe and arrival to the river mouth by an open boat from Tofino, not by floatplane to Megin Lake as most were thought to have arrived.

Joined by Randy Stetzer of Portland, Oregon, the four of us looked out from the Tofino dock onto the gray expanse of sky and water awaiting a decision to load and cast off. Six foot swells rolled ominous – white spume blowing off their crests. But the rain diminished from a steady stinging pelt to a light mist after a three hour wait. Although the sky remained leaden with black gnarls and streaks, the swells were down to three feet with lengthening spaces between. It was nearly four o'clock; if we waited any longer we would have too little time to reach the mouth of the Megin. Any better weather break may not occur on the west coast of Vancouver Island in our allotted ten days. We each nodded with a vote to go.

Next day, tired, sore, and sweating from paddling, pulling and pushing the gear-laden canoes upstream seven miles, we turned a sudden bend and there was the late afternoon sun on the saw-tooth of white mountains jutting behind Megin Lake. Fifteen minutes later we found the shake lean-too overlooking the lake beneath 200 foot high cedars – the Megin Log awaiting on the plank table.

Melody on Deschutes River in 1998.

Each dawn was greeted by the yodel of loon and the ghostly flap of unseen raven wings cutting through the forest mist. Throughout the days came the dull throb of drumming grouse. As I drew at my pipe during long evenings of lantern light and Teacher's scotch, Don and Jim told us of their snorkeling adventures with the Roderick Haig-Brown Fly Fishing Association to determine diminished numbers of steelhead on Vancouver Island rivers. In the background came the calls of a barred owl softened by the forest filter of hanging lichen.

In memory of the splendor of the Megin, and the man who had inspired the stories long into our wilderness nights, that summer of 1983 Randy and I spread the prophetic vision of Haig-Brown's snorkeling to illuminate the level of wild steelhead depletion on southern Washington's Wind River. Two years later we extended the snorkels to the Washougal and East Fork Lewis rivers, all of which contributed to an eventual Threatened listing under the Endangered Species Act for Lower Columbia River wild steelhead. My son, John, began as a 12-year-old the following summer. In 1999 he began snorkel surveys for the Wild Salmon Center on the Olympic Peninsula's Hoh River. Snorkeling 50 - 150 miles each year, the data helped identify priority conservation areas as part of the Western Rivers Conservancy's dedicated effort to purchase and protect more than 6,800 acres of private lands that are now managed by the Hoh River Trust.

Revelations from snorkeling have led to its spread as a tool of science – call it extreme biology – to protect fish, rivers, and related wildlife, and even shifts in the way some of us individually perceive ourselves in a larger web of life that would have brought a knowing grin from a Chinese fisherman of long ago.

Bill McMillan, Sr. & Washougal River steelhead in 1956.

The pages that follow provide the images my son, John, and I have recorded through the medium of photography in lives largely spent on rivers as fishermen, naturalists, biologists – men struck by the wonder of the life of rivers. Rivers are the calendar to our lives from which we tell time.

It was in my 20s, during national and personal turmoil, that Roderick Haig-Brown's *A River Never Sleeps* came to be a "Bible" read over and over again, its passages rippling through my mind like a Buddhist chant – like the ceaseless sound of water over rocks. When marriage came two years after enduring that dark year of American history in 1968, I knew the quest for the personal detachment of peace to build a family around was that of life lived on a river. The Washougal River became that subsequent home where Melody and John spent childhood hours largely nurtured by a river – fear of wind and flood in winter, the endless playmates of pool and riffle in summer.

Where I may have failed, the river did not. It nurtured both children into strong, bold, and idealistic adults with reverence for life and related human responsibility to sustain life. Melody's came to be expressed through care and protection of domestic animals, John's for wild fish and birds.

This is a book that expresses the love John and I found for the mystery of life as represented by Northwest rivers and its wild fish. Although the photos rarely depict Melody, the image of her behind them is forever visible to us. Swimming, diving, floating, fishing, wading, hiking, watching – she was our continual partner who had to endure us and provide the example to become better than ourselves. We all grew up together as I learned the depth of Wordsworth's line:

Bill & John on Deschutes River in 1972.

"The child is father of the man."

One message we hope to convey is that the rivers never slept in the era of Haig-Brown's earliest Northwest experiences due to the great abundance of life they sustained, an abundance largely perpetuated by salmon that depended on their own returning multitudes, as much so dead as alive.

A 2001 study found that at least part of the lifecycle of 138 species of wildlife in Washington and Oregon is associated with salmon. It has been theorized that forestation after glaciations followed salmon nutrients upland from Northwest river valleys into mountain headwaters due to animals carrying and defecating them. Many species are thought to have a co-evolutionary relationship with salmon stimulating both terrestrial and aquatic food webs that knit water and land together.

The question is, will Northwest rivers continue to remain awake with perpetual life; or will their encounters with modern humanity increasingly narrow the life they support with resulting sleep?

This book is our celebration of the 103rd year after Haig-Brown's birth and the ethic of responsibility for rivers and anadromous fish he unwittingly birthed. It is also a celebration of the love of wild waters my father, a canoeist and fisherman, instilled stemming from his childhood growing up on Oregon's Clackamas River in the early 1900s.

John was born color blind, I was not. Oddly, much of my photography is the B&W medium while John's is color. Our resulting photos tell the differing stories as we alternate through 12 months of the year.

January

When the Steelhead Now Enter

A female steelhead donning the silvery chainmail of anadromy, and while she is fresh from the sea, her protruding vent and bulging belly indicate she will spawn within the month.

Beginning ten days after the winter solstice, January denotes the start of our calendar. Calendars are systems of timekeeping that define the beginning, length, and divisions of a year. While calendars based on a tabular array of days are a staple in most modern cultures, they do not adequately represent the shifting mosaic of climate and river conditions, fish and wildlife movements that give framework to my life's expectations. Instead, I have come to visualize each month as a series of memories shaped by a magnetic need to observe, understand, and interact with nature, especially with rivers and fish.

Snow trims the margins of a rainforest river, a few days later the snow was gone and the river was flooding.

In my calendar of memories, rivers and salmon are analogues of time. Each month represents a temporal place along a continuum of relatively predictable physical and biological patterns. Of course, patterns can vary greatly between regions. Most of my fishing and natural history experience in January has come from rivers draining the coast ranges and the western slopes of the Cascade Mountains in Oregon and Washington. In these areas, I associate January with a physical dichotomy in climate and river flows and a biological transition from the end of the fall salmon to the arrival of wild winter steelhead. Given its proximity to the solstice and its transitional nature, I view January as an ecological junction in the natural rhythm of rivers and salmon.

Between the wet winter darkness of December and February's hint of spring, January conditions cannot be singularly described. In some years, cold rainstorms pound the rivers for weeks, only ever briefly retreating to allow for a few precious moments of sunshine. I remember standing on a terrace overlooking a rainforest river during a particularly ferocious early January flood. Twenty feet below me, the once gentle stream of summer roared through a steep boulder alley in a series of dense, brown rolling waves. It was raining so hard that I could barely see 100 feet – dependent on sound and smell more than sight. Cobbles and boulders rolled downstream rattling like hollow bowling balls through a concrete tube, and the dense air held the pungent, piney-sweet fragrance of freshly splintered trees devoured by the flood.

Days later the flows receded and I was waist deep fishing a run formed by a Spruce tree that held its ground against the flood's brutish force. I caught my first winter steelhead of the year that day: a small bright hen. The window was short lived. The rains returned the next day and rendered most of the month unfishable.

White and curled alder limbs contrasted against bright green moss and aqua-colored water provide a rainforest backdrop deep in the Siletz River gorge.

In other years, January may be a month of snowstorms or prolonged periods of dry, intense cold. When this happens on coastal rivers, frost and ice can frame the river's margins for days and the mountaintops may remain pillowy white for weeks. In contrast, streams draining the western slopes of the Cascade Mountains may freeze over almost entirely, flows shrouded by the convergence of surface ice and anchor ice – headwaters snowbound for months. It was during such a year that Dougan Falls on the Washougal River froze solid for two weeks, the whole river nearly coming to a halt. And so it is with January, a contrast in climate manifested in rivers as either flood or ice.

A low snow line on the Hoh River near the Olympic National Park, an area that is nearly pristine and protects over 65% of the watershed from future development.

While the weather of January may be dichotomous, biologically it is a transitional month. It covers the last throes of fall's spawning salmon and the arrival of winter steelhead just beginning their reproductive journey. Although some salmon remain alive, the dead outnumber the living. Carcasses in various pieces and states of decay are ubiquitous along the cobbled stream banks and vegetated benches. Skulls, spines, ribs, jaws, and bits of fins are most common. Each piece is a reminder that I am observing the final act of the salmon cycle, the end of their annual evolutionary performance in the ecological theater of rivers.

An Elwha River bull trout plump from feeding after spawning earlier during fall.

Beyond climate, river flow, and salmon, January is best epitomized by the arrival of winter-run steelhead. From my perspective in time as a 39-year-old fisherman, January has generally marked the start of the winter steelhead season. Although a few steelhead can arrive in November, and more commonly December, the more consistent time of wild steelhead entry is now January. This may not have always been the case. There is evidence that January was once the peak entry time of winter steelhead in many streams, rather than the start.

My father's obsessively thorough reviews of fishery data from the mid 1800s through the 1950s indicate that our view of steelhead has been reshaped by the shifting baseline syndrome, a term first described by Daniel Pauly in his 1995 paper "Anecdotes and the Shifting Baseline Syndrome of Fisheries," published in the journal *Trends in Ecology and Evolution*. The term "shifting baseline" denotes the common fisheries science failure to identify a valid baseline for the abundance, productivity, distribution, and diversity of a fish species prior to industrial level human exploitation. The 'baselines' commonly used depict the era each new generation of biologists inherit and are not historically old enough to prevent being skewed by prior cumulative human influences on fish and their habitat.

The concept of a shifting baseline is particularly applicable to the entry timing of winter steelhead in the Pacific Northwest. For example, dad found that from 1934 to 1959 (prior to the modern hatchery program) over 90% of the steelhead caught in tribal fisheries from ten

The motto for male steelhead is 'better early than late' as most tend to enter rivers earlier in the season than females so that they can fight for the first choice in mates and spawning territories.

Boldt Case rivers in Washington State occurred in December, January, and February. Similarly, Washington Department of Game's sport-catch data from 1948 to 1959 indicated that wild-steelhead returns were dominated by December through February catch. Unfortunately, the early run timing component of our wild winter-run steelhead in many watersheds has been nearly eradicated for a variety of reasons. A faulty baseline may be one. Because many contemporary anglers are not familiar with the historical run timing data, it is now commonly accepted that January is the start of the wild winter steelhead season, no longer the peak. This has not always been the case and it is important to understand what has occurred.

The extent to which the run timing of winter steelhead has been altered is not clear. Surely, the entry and spawn timing varied considerably among rivers in response to environmental and biological regimes. January may indeed have represented the start of winter steelhead entry in some places, but certainly not everywhere. The bottom line is that what we see today does not necessarily match what existed just 50-60 years ago, let alone over 100 years ago. The shifting experiences among generations have resulted in varying expectations, such that each generation redefines what is "natural." Within this context, January is not only transitional from a salmon and steelhead point of view, but it is also transitional to generations of anglers and scientists. To each generation January has meant something different for steelhead and that is likely to continue.

Moss drapes an old log that has fallen over the river, an indicator of the lush growth potential in coastal rainforests.

The skull of a hook-nosed coho salmon entombed in sand after a flood.

If we fail to reverse the shifting baseline syndrome, the biological patterns of January will continue changing through my lifetime, just as it did for my father and grandfather. To my grandfather, January was the peak of winter steelhead angling. To me, it represents the start. Perhaps in 30-40 years, January will mean to winter steelhead what December now means, a month largely devoid of wild fish. In that case, February will come to denote the arrival of winter steelhead. In some Washington rivers it already does. If changes continue to outpace biological recovery the symbolism of our natural calendars lose their value. A perspective that accounts for winter steelhead 100 years ago and that of the future 100 years from now from a single temporal place is the only way to ensure that the symbols we have today remain the symbols of tomorrow. Without doing so our attachment to time will continually be lost and replaced. After all, how much value can a symbol have if the experience is not shared by overlapping generations?

North Cascade Mountains viewed from Skagit River, Washington.

Water ouzel (aka American dipper) on Elwha River.

February

The Water Ouzel's Song

Although there are wet and dreary days in February, sometimes bitter days with ice rimming the pools and trudges through foot deep snow, for some reason they are lost to memory. More remembered is February light on broken water accompanied by the cascading song of the water ouzel – a gay spirited little bird that flits from rock to rock doing the continuous bob and weave of a boxer on the ropes. And there are memories of nightfall with frog-song near and far across the meadows and swamps after a couple of 50-degree days rouse them from winter's sleep. From a log in the alder bottoms a ruffed grouse may burst into first breeding season drum – regrettably, a sound so low in pitch my ears have not discerned it for ten years beyond the pulse of it in the blood of my memory. Each time while passing through sunlit white alder trunks lining the edge of green water there is the fond hope to hear it one last time.

Finney Creek alder bottom, Skagit River basin.

And despite the many years of fishing February rivers in the focus on catching steelhead, it is not the fishing I remember either. Far upstream in the headwater reaches of certain coastal rivers and creeks wild summer-run steelhead that have overcome waterfalls and steep canyon cascades silently work their way into tributary creeks as little as 8-10 feet wide to commence spawning, sometimes as early as January, but more commonly February. It was initially fishing that attracted me to steelhead, and to catch them one has to learn something of them. But steelhead fishing does not take one to those small secret places where they were birthed and will spawn. And for me, fishing was not enough in the limitations of what one can more fully experience with these aquatic animals.

As Roderick Haig-Brown found when anadromous fish returns on the Campbell River began to alter due to dams and electric power generation, fishing alone was no longer sufficiently fulfilling. He needed to learn more of the fish than a rod and reel would tell him in the desire to protect these animals that fishing had brought him to … well … love. It is the only word that adequately conveys what he must have felt for them. It spurred him to find alternatives to learn more about them and to speak on their behalf with an increasing transition from recreational angler to ichthyologist and conservationist.

Wild female summer-run steelhead digging spawning nest, Silver Creek of upper Washougal River.

Dougan Creek bedrock cascade that selects
for passage of smaller steelhead.

Having fished the Washougal River since a boy of 12 in 1956, and having come to live on it as a young man in 1970, by the time of 1979 it was apparent that wild steelhead were not only in decline but entire life history characteristics had altered or completely disappeared. The example of Haig-Brown's progression from that of a fisherman to that of conservationist and hobby ichthyologist would no longer let me merely fish. In the spring of 1979 I began to follow the summer-run steelhead upstream into their spawning tributaries.

One of these tributaries, Dougan Creek, is a fascinating example of steelhead adaptation that makes use of every square foot of stream. About 200 yards from its entry to the upper Washougal River, it drops over a basalt face in a thin sheet of water with a variable 45-60 degree slope about 50 feet in length. By any measure of physics or logic it should deny upstream migration. However, during an exploratory search in February of 1981, a female steelhead was found on a spawning nest three-quarters of a mile above the cascades. Subsequent surveys over the next dozen years found two more lone female steelhead, each on spawning nests well above the cascade. These female steelhead were relatively small in size, from 4 to 7 pounds each. The only male ever observed was a dark-colored resident rainbow of 8-10 inches in company with one of the larger female steelhead. Small resident males may have provided all three of the female

February's green candelabra of Indian Plum along Washougal River.

steelhead with mates they otherwise would not have had. This was my initial enlightenment into the secret world of steelhead mating that son John would more fully reveal with underwater photography 20-25 years later.

Dougan Creek provided other revelations. Between the cascades and entry to the Washougal River there were only three patches of spawning gravel tucked into hollows of dark basalt laid across the land by volcanism eons earlier. Yet, these few patches of available gravel supported annual returns of 15-30 wild steelhead as found in twelve years of recorded observations. Unlike the few small steelhead and the occasional sea-run cutthroat of 15-20 inches found above the cascades, the steelhead sighted below the cascades could be as large as 18 pounds, nearly three times the maximum of those above. The cascades apparently selected for steelhead of smaller size – their smaller mass and greater percentage of tail bite in the thin sheet of water perhaps a main determinant for upstream ascendance. Only these smaller anadromous fish were found to access this particular habitat niche in the Washougal basin.

However, between the mid 1950s and the late 1970s, smaller sized steelhead returning to the Washougal basin were largely eliminated, leaving habitat niches like Dougan Creek nearly vacant of steelhead productivity. Initially a most discouraging discovery, over the years new hope has

Newly emerged Chinook fry dewatered below Baker River dam operations on the Skagit River, but one of the factors limiting wild salmon, steelhead, and bull trout productivity in Washington's Skagit basin.

bloomed for their eventual recovery, which may rest in the few resident rainbow upstream of the cascade that cohabit with a larger population of coastal cutthroat. It is increasingly being found that some seemingly "resident" rainbow trout upstream of barriers can migrate downstream to the ocean with resulting steelhead returns when conditions are right for their survival. This is one of the adaptive strengths of rainbow/steelhead. It has allowed them to inhabit the greatest native range of Pacific salmon and trout around the North Pacific Rim from southern Kamchatka to mid Mexico. John's recent research at Oregon State University now sheds light on what triggers life history switches in rainbow/steelhead – a combination of differences in growth and whole-body fat content in the first year of life.

All along North America's west coast steelhead initiate spawning in February – sometimes January – and it is the peak of spawning for migratory cutthroat trout. They work silently up into tributary streams where Indian plumb's bright green candelabras of new leaf glow from winter-dark forests. The riverbanks are lined by osier, suddenly red-stemmed with rising sap, canopied beneath the drape of alder limbs dripping with maroon catkins. Along with the movements of steelhead and cutthroat these are the West Coast's first heralds of spring – life's evidence of renewal at the retreating edge of winter. These are the indicators that draw me from the woodstove of our Skagit River house to walk for hours along near-by creeks in our mutual celebrations. And for seven years I traveled to Seattle one day each week in February

Bull trout gorged on pink salmon fry on Skagit River in February 2010 from a larger than average pink salmon return in 2009. All aquatic life in the river greatly benefited through the increased nutrients of eggs and decomposing carcasses.

to document the mystery of wild cutthroat trout moving out of Lake Washington to spawn in Thornton Creek with remarkable abundance in an urban environment toxic to coho salmon and otherwise reduced aquatic life.

It is also a time when anadromous bull trout migrate into stream systems to feed on Chinook and pink salmon fry which can emerge from gravel nests as early as January, but increasingly in February and March. Bull trout are nomadic and on the northwest Olympic coast have been found to stray from tagged captures in the Hoh River into small systems like Kallaloch and Ruby creeks – systems where neither Chinook nor pink salmon are now known to return. They are apparently drawn there by other feeding opportunities. Bull trout are a char and for many years were considered one and the same with Dolly Varden. This altered in the late 1980s when West Coast scientists reclassified bull trout and Dolly Varden as separate species. Bull trout along the Washington coast and Puget Sound are now thought to be mostly anadromous and Dolly Varden, what few are left, are limited to a few resident populations in headwater areas. Bull trout are listed in Washington as Threatened under the Endangered Species Act, yet Dolly Varden are not – an interesting contradiction where bull trout are far more abundant in most instances. What the historic distribution once was between the two species in Washington is not clearly known, but their abundance in Puget Sound reported in the 1850s was staggering, apparently dependent on even more staggering returns of salmon at that time.

The Olympic Mountains overlook the lower Elwha River, the right bank of which features a series of engineered logjams constructed by the Lower Elwha Tribe to improve fish habitat.

Right: Glowing-red cheeks, a red stripe and thick shoulders indicate the onset of dimorphism and full maturity in this male steelhead. His vivid colors are fleeting, within a few days or weeks they will fade as his body deteriorates after successive rounds of fighting other males for the right to the dominant position alongside any female of his choosing.

March

Climatic Tantrums and Gladiators

I sat down to write this chapter after returning from fishing my favorite stream on the Oregon coast. The weather forecast was heavy rains and strong steady winds with occasional gusts to 40 mph. Indeed, I thought. Not to be deterred, I scrambled down a steep hillside and upstream through brush along the bank to a gravelly glide dotted with boulders every five to fifteen yards. Waist deep, drenched by the rainforest downpour, my fly swung through the run. My dog Honey, pouting with shrugged shoulders, was hiding under the hollowed-out bole of a big leaf maple. She does not like the rain.

Low-gradient stream meanders through alder and maple forests on the Oregon coast, a favorite habitat type for over-wintering juvenile coho.

After thirty minutes of deluge I felt a tap-tap and the line gradually pulled taut. At the apex of the tug I set the hook to the inside bank and the rod bucked with the deep headshakes of a larger steelhead. After two reel-emptying runs and a couple of leaps, I beached the fish fifty yards downstream on a patch of gravel perched precariously on a bedrock ledge.

It was a male with strong shoulders, a light green back, opaque black spots, and two blood red stripes, one on its side and another on its belly. Its tail was unusually broad and long, like a fan, and its adipose so large that it looked like a glistening spotted mushroom. There were a few scars on its caudal area, presumably from fighting other males for access to spawning females. As I released the fish and it disappeared into the green depths, it started hailing. Fifteen minutes later as I waded back out into the river to swing through the run again, the hail stopped and the sun came out. Though not the chrome knight of early winter, the fish and the weather symbolized my angling experience in March – a scarred, double red-striped male steelhead caught during a weather tantrum.

A long run on the Quinalt River stoically continues downstream as the remnants of a high-elevation snow storm pass over the tips of the Olympics. After another snow storm and a rain-on-snow event, the channel flipped and the run disappeared only a week after this photo.

While my symbol for March is a large fully mature male steelhead, the condition and extent of maturity among steelhead are often quite diverse. Bright males and females are common in early March, but by late March I begin to encounter a higher rate of spawned out females (kelts) and most of the larger males are displaying full spawning colors. This is probably because steelhead spawning activity increases sharply through the month, resulting in an array of steelhead in various states of physical condition ranging from sea-lice carrying females to fungus-ridden bucks on their last legs. The variation in steelhead imagery underscores that March is a temporal place of diversity along the steelhead continuum. Thus, the large male is not necessarily representative of all March steelhead. Instead, using a Christmas analogy, the blood red-striped male is like the star on the top of the tree while the other steelhead are the ornaments.

Particularly interesting to me is the distinction in male images that I conjure when recalling my angling experiences in rain- and glacially-dominated watersheds. In watersheds where monthly river flow patterns are dominated by rainfall, rivers tend to run relatively clear and the

The reward for a long day of surface fishing on an unseasonably warm March afternoon: a fresh female steelhead that ambushed a waking Steelhead Caddis.

water temperatures have increased compared to January and February. Consequently, steelhead spawning activity is well underway. Due to a combination of increased light penetration into the clearer water, increased water temperatures, and heavy female spawning activity, large males in these streams tend to be vividly colored. They also often don bite marks and the tips of their ventral-side fins may be slightly worn from spawning and fighting in the shallow riffles where females prefer to spawn. Despite the scars, these males are in wonderful condition from the perspective of admiring females – they are brightly colored and they have established social dominance through aggression.

In contrast to rain-dominated streams, vividly colored males appear to be more common in April than in March in watersheds where stream flows are driven by snow or rain-and-snow. This probably occurs for two reasons, which I overly simplify to make my point. First, fish coloration is partially controlled by penetration of light through the water column, which is limited in March compared to April in glacial streams because of turbidity. Second, the spawn timing of female steelhead tends to peak about a month later in glacial streams compared to rain-dominated streams because of differences in thermal regimes. Because of the differences in light exposure and spawn timing, and the close association between expression of male spawning colors and female spawning activity, March males in glacial rivers often display the faded red and green colors of an old flag.

*A small coastal river basks in the warming rays of spring, a photoperiod shift
that helps stimulate the spawning activity of steelhead.*

Whether vibrant or faded, it is appropriate that March males display their sexual prowess with red. The month was named after Mars, the Roman god of war symbolized by red. In human psychology, red is associated with fire, blood, anger, and passion. Each time I land a double red-striped male, I am immediately taken by the notion of an old battle-wagon – an individual that has been through the wars of mating, a competition fostered by the instinctive desire to breed. In this vein, the male steelhead donning blood-red armor represents the apex gladiator in the aqueous arena of rivers.

Of course, steelhead are but one part of the biological rhythms and natural vitality of March. The arrival of the solstice and increased day length prompts a strong climatic and biological response. Humans identified these patterns long ago, as their survival depended on it. For example, March signified the start of the Roman year because it coincided with the onset of the growing season. In fact, the Roman god Mars was initially viewed as the overseer of fertility and vegetation. It was only later on that he became so strongly associated with war and bloodshed. Almost forgotten in our modern culture, Great Britain recognized March 25 as the beginning of the New Year until 1752. Following this tradition, I too associate March with renewed life, although the physical and biological patterns are specific to the places I have lived.

The gladiator, a ripe male steelhead with flush-red gill plates and cranky snout.

In watersheds draining Puget Sound and the Olympic Peninsula, March is best described with the old saying "in like a lion, out like a lamb." The Oregon Coast is similar, although the timing of particular biological events appears to occur slightly earlier, probably due to its lower latitude. In these areas, early March is marked by the last roaring storms of winter, which may include devastating rain-on-snow flood events. As the month progresses, the duration of intense rainstorms decreasingly evolves into infrequent bursts of thunder and sputtering fits of rain accompanied by warming sun breaks. The exaggerated spikes in winter stream flow ebb into a rolling ensemble of pulsing flows and increasing temperatures. By the end of March, the once barren cobble/boulder stream bottoms begin to accumulate algae and large brown mayflies abundantly hatch. Stimulated by rain and increasing exposure to solar radiation, the rivers are invigorated with fresh life.

The river banks are brimming with activity by late March. Schools of juvenile salmon and steelhead emerge from winter hiding, competing, and darting around in search of food.

A late-March sunset at the mouth of a coastal river where its last riffle meanders into the ocean, a beautiful place to sit and watch the occasional school of steelhead porpoise as they enter freshwater to begin their spawning journey.

Juvenile coho are especially common in off-channel sloughs and wetland ponds where mating newts are ubiquitous, careless, and single-minded. Chinook are out too, but are a bit more wary than coho. Adult steelhead are spawning and the eggs of their earlier spawning counterparts remain buried in the gravel. Water ouzels flitter into and out of the water, incessantly bobbing, with males courting females like kamikaze pilots in an aerial duel. Newly arrived swallows dart, glide, and dive over the river. In the riparian forest canopy and understory, the avian symphony ranges from the raucous, scolding rattle of the belted kingfisher to the melodious serenade of the courting winter wren. Along the river and in its floodplain, trees, shrubs, and flowers are starting to bloom, painting the forest and forest floor with a fresh tinge of greens, yellows and whites. As the first act of spring winds to a close, the dampness of the lion's roar begins to fade away as the warming rays of sun and the vitality of nurturing water start priming the biological pump for the coming spring and summer.

April

Rivers Determined by Waterfalls

Dog-toothed violet along
Washougal River in April.

Dry Falls of the Columbia River where the largest river in the world once ran.

The Columbia River is the most interesting river basin in the world from the standpoint of its geomorphology. Repeated layers of volcanic basalt over hundreds of thousands of years were followed by retreating Ice Age blowout floods 15,000-12,000 years ago. These floods resulted in the largest river ever known to run across the planet traveling at 50 mph and reshaping 16,000 square miles of landscape. Evidence of the Columbia's massive scale during some 40 floods when the ice dams broke is still provided at the stunning expanse of Dry Falls. Farther downstream the floods were 700-800 feet up the walls of the Columbia Gorge and 400 feet deep from its outlet to the Pacific.

The response of salmonids in their adaptations to the dramatic alterations after the Missoula floods resulted in peak anadromous fish abundance and distribution at the time of David Thompson's exploration to the Columbia headwaters in 1807. Thompson, employed by the North West Company, brought the beaver fur trade with him. The fur trade largely eradicated beaver from the Columbia/Snake basin by 1840, with dramatic alterations to the hydrology of melting snows off the mountains to the sea and outright losses of some of the most productive salmon rearing habitat beaver ponds provide. The Euro-American quests for profit off natural resources began to alter the Columbia's aquatic life almost from the get-go. Nevertheless, on a larger and older scale, salmon eradication from large geographic areas was the ironic driver of what North America's Pacific salmonids became at the time of their great abundance in the early 1800s. They are animals well adapted to survival in the long term from catastrophic events – at least those of the past.

Fish passage denied at Dougan Falls in winter ice, high-velocity flood, and summer-fall drought.

The primary line of adaptive demarcation in the Columbia River basin was historic Celilo Falls, since 1957 inundated below backwaters of The Dalles Dam. What the Columbia basin was before the Lake Missoula floods spewed out of Montana is largely unknown. That ancient landscape was swept to sea, or remains as sediment in the agricultural soil of the Willamette Valley and other areas filled by vast lakes in the Ice Age aftermaths until they eventually drained.

Dougan Falls at optimal passage conditions for wild summer-run steelhead from late April to early June.

But it is known that Celilo Falls was a creation of the great floods. The salmon/steelhead that eventually recolonized the Columbia had to adapt to differing landscapes known as eco-regions – wet coastal forests below Celilo, arid inland expanses above. The physical barrier of the falls helped to enforce this climatic separation between anadromous fish populations. For instance winter-run steelhead could not return above Celilo. The lowest flows occurred in winter and left the falls at its maximum height. Very cold water temperatures further limited passage. Temperature strictly determines the activity level of cold-blooded animals. Water temperatures below 45° F minimize fish athleticism. Anadromous fish passage at Celilo was denied from November through March due to cold inland winters that keep precipitation locked up as snow or ice – flows low and cold. Subsequent anadromous fish passage at Celilo Falls from April through October included varying flow levels and waterfall heights that determined which species and stocks could pass month by month with eventual dispersal in the mainstem and tributaries:

Spring Chinook	April-May
Summer Chinook	June-July
Fall Chinook	August-September
Coho	July-September
Sockeye	May-July
Likely chum	now unknown
Summer steelhead	June-October
Perhaps some pink	now unknown

Small 23-inch wild summer-run steelhead perfection: once common to the Washougal River in mid-summer months they are now virtually extinct (photo in early July of 1979).

Wild upper Washougal River steelhead: victims of dynamiting, spearing, snagging,
and historic over-harvest; and as many as 200 were annually killed in the
Washougal Salmon Hatchery holding ponds until the latter 1980s.

Although Celilo Falls is presently beneath The Dalles Dam pool, the Washougal River 80 miles downstream still provides a geomorphologic example of what may have been the greatest rainbow/steelhead diversity per basin size in the species' range. The Washougal basin is divided into numerous habitat niches by ten major mainstem waterfalls, four more on its North Fork, numerous smaller tributary falls and cascades, and shallow bedrock expanses throughout. At least one race or stock of steelhead ascends past each of the mainstem and North Fork falls – fourteen in all – as well as beyond many of the other highly selective barriers on smaller tributaries. The historical range of fall Chinook, coho, and chum salmon was much more limited as restricted by these same waterfalls. It is now thought fall Chinook and coho did not return above Salmon Falls until it was laddered in 1957, although there is no history source that denies the potential they may have gone as far as Dougan Falls. Original wild stocks of fall Chinook and coho may no longer exist, both depleted or eradicated by prolific hatchery programs and altered habitat. Chum salmon are now extinct beyond occasional strays, eliminated by increased toxic effluent from a pulp mill at its mouth during the 1940s and vast quantities of gravel mined from the lower mile of river bed where they once spawned in greatest abundance – likely tens of thousands in the 1800s.

Although wild rainbow/steelhead remain, their historic numbers and life history diversity have been reduced since the construction of Skamania Hatchery in 1956. The hatchery took virtually all the returning North Fork summer-runs for broodstock in its initial 3-4 years of operation and subsequently increased harvest and rearing pressures on wild steelhead. Selective practices at the hatchery varied between 1956 to the early 1980s: 1) early spawning, 2) males 34 inches or longer, and females 30 inches or longer, and 3) smaller adults after selection for large size eliminated that entire life history – but subsequently failed due to prior eradication of smaller steelhead.

Nevertheless, genetics analysis in the 1990s found at least four remaining wild stocks – two summer-run and two winter-run. What the original genetic diversity once was will never be known. However, steelhead life history diversity as evidenced by my experiences since 1956 and from listening to the characteristics of steelhead that returned there from the memories of reputable men one or two generations older than I, clearly indicated considerable loss by the early 1990s:

Life History Type

Run time		Morphology	Basin area	Status
Early winter-run	Nov-Feb	6-22 lb/thick	Salmon Falls-Dougan Falls	remnant
Late winter-run	Mar-May	2-20 lb/avg	Below Salmon Falls	depressed
Very late winter-run	May-June	4-15 lb/avg	Above Dougan Falls	remnant
Early summer-run	Mar-May	3-16 lb/lean	NF & above Dougan Falls	remnant
Mid summer-run	June-Aug	1.5-5 lb/lean	NF & above Dougan Falls	extinct
Late summer-run	Sep-Oct	4-30 lb/thick	Salmon Falls-Silver Falls	remnant
Estuarine	Anytime	14-18"/avg	Unknown	extinct
Upper resident	none	10-22"/thick	Above Salmon Falls	healthy
Lower resident	none	10-22"/thick	Below Salmon Falls	remnant
Tributary resident	none	4-12"/avg	Throughout	healthy

Dougan Falls remains a critical point for largely excluding hatchery steelhead from entry. If it were modified for easier passage it would no longer isolate the wild summer-run population above from hatchery steelhead interactions. Dougan Falls seasonally alters from that of being locked beneath ice in severe winters, to that of a brown torrent in flood, to that of insurmountable little spigots of water plummeting off its basalt face from mid June through September. Ideal passage flows most predictably occur from late April to early June. The once dominant early summer-run with lower river passage that historically peaked in early April maximized the likelihood of arriving at Dougan Falls in that time period. Remnant returns of that early summer-run remain – the athletic superstars of fish capable of leaping falls 12-14 feet high.

The Washougal River, its fish and falls, have a deep personal meaning for John and me. On Mother's Day each year for 20 years I went to Dougan Falls to watch and photograph the steelhead leaping there after picking wild flower bouquets. On Easter morning of 1956, my father gave the gift of my first spinning reel and rod. Only slightly embarrassed, he got up at 4:00 a.m. that morning to test the rod and reel resulting in his first Washougal River steelhead – a long, lean summer-run athlete of 36 inches and 14.5 lb. He asked me to take a photograph, the first I ever took (blurry as it may be). The sight of that silver and black fish would haunt me for over two years until finally hooking my own. Eighteen years later I put John, age three, on my back and waded him to a Washougal River island where I hooked a steelhead and quickly handed him the rod. His tenacity to hang onto the bucking rod and whirling reel resulted in a stranger's applause from the near-by bridge when the miniature fisherman reeled the thrashing catch to beach – memories of a river, now bittersweet for both of us as it fades into the distance of purpose once served.

Klickitat River: wild spring Chinook nearing extinction from fishway construction and hatchery impacts.

Wallowa Lake in April ice-out where a hatchery dam in the early 1900s eradicated sockeye salmon.

May

Guards and Sneakers

May is a crossroads for steelhead, their juveniles are emerging and spawned-out adults are perishing. Here a bald eagle feeds on a steelhead that recently died from the rigors of spawning.

The dust settles after this sculpin captured this steelhead that was 2-4 weeks old. Piscivorous fish of all species tend to capture their prey head first. Soon after the photo the sculpin swam forward a few feet and rammed the tail of the fish into a rock several times to push it further down its throat.

In the coastal rivers of Oregon and Washington, May is the time of year when the river blooms with spawning steelhead. Of course, the timing of steelhead spawning can be highly variable. Roderick Haig-Brown said it best in *A River Never Sleeps*, "Generalizations about fish are shoddy and dangerous." For example, he observed steelhead spawning into July in the Campbell River watershed. I too have found wild steelhead spawning over a protracted period, ranging from early January through July on the Olympic Peninsula. In any given year the spawn timing depends largely on water temperature, but May consistently provides prime conditions for watching spawning steelhead: good water clarity and frequent spawning activity.

Most spawning steelhead return to freshwater for the first time after spending one to three years in the ocean. Mixed with the first-time spawners are repeat spawning steelhead, nearly all of which are female, that spent one or more additional years recovering in the ocean after spawning previously in freshwater. Remarkably, some individuals have been documented to spawn six times in the Pacific Northwest and up to ten times in Russia. Although the current extent of repeat

Tailout of a coastal river basks in the fresh growth and nurturing light of spring.

A school of winter steelhead holds in a deep pool as they wait out a prolonged period of cold weather prior to spawning.

spawning is low compared to historic estimates, repeat spawning individuals are present in most, if not all, steelhead populations. In May steelhead of various shapes, sizes, and colors can be easily observed spawning in shallow riffles, tail-outs, and channel margins. Their behavior can be quite raucous and often attracts the attention of other fish, mammals and birds.

Because of the opportunities for observation in May, I have increasingly shifted my attention from angling to documenting steelhead behavior. Of course, this was not always the case. As a boy, I spent May fishing for summer steelhead on the Washougal River more often driven by catching than observing. I still occasionally fish in May for late arriving winter steelhead, fresh spring Chinook, and if angling is allowed, coastal cutthroat. All of my angling experiences have been rewarding and contribute to my calendar of memories. Nonetheless, fishing has seldom provided the insight into steelhead behavior that focused observation and underwater videography has.

On moving to Forks, Washington in the late 1990s I initiated a personal and professional journey to document and describe the spawning behavior of steelhead and resident rainbow trout in the Sol Duc and Calawah rivers. Although I observed a wide range of behaviors one memory burns brighter than others. On a particularly warm morning in May 2002 I hiked a couple of miles through clear-cuts and salmonberry thickets to access a particularly bountiful spawning area. Sweating like a pig, I heard a great commotion at the river. I dropped my backpack and ran through the last ten yards of salmonberry to see what was happening. Ten feet away three fighting steelhead had nearly beached themselves on a gravel bar. A large male of about 19 pounds was thrashing in four inches of water as another male, of about 12 pounds, gripped his tail. The third male, of about 9 pounds, was biting the tail of the 12-pound male. Despite the precarious

This post-spawn female steelhead has black-spot disease, which is caused by parasitic turbellarian flatworms. The parasite can kill fish and is more common in streams with elevated water temperatures, which could become a more extensive problem with climate change.

exposure, each refused to let go of the other. In this test of dominance, the writhing chain of steelhead broke when the 12-pound male eventually lost his grip on the largest fish. Perhaps frustrated at his own inability to shake the smallest male, he turned and reciprocated the action, the result of which was two fish biting each other's tail in a whirling dervish. It looked like a dog chasing its tail. Eventually, they worked out of the shallows and into the main current where the fight continued downstream until I could no longer see them.

I do not know who won the fight, but observing their antics heightened my intensity and anticipation more than angling ever had. The tailout of the pool was alive with spawning steelhead. I grabbed my journal, popped open a can of soda and took a seat on a mossy spruce log. I had a free ticket to the ecological theater of behavior.

Over the next five hours, I documented a range of behaviors. A typical observation included one large dominant male flanking a female excavating a nest. The dominant male is referred to as a "guard" because he attempts to monopolize access to females by using aggression. Alongside the spawning pair would be one to six sub-dominant 'sneaker' males that were smaller or in poorer condition. During mating, a female would dip her vent into the nest pocket, arch her spine, and as she deposited eggs, the sub-dominant males would dart alongside the pair to sneak fertilizations. These events were astonishingly diverse. I watched as many as seven males attempt to fertilize one female during a single mating. From above water, the mating appeared like a chorus line of gaping white mouths trailed by a floating cloud of sperm. That day, the competition among males for females was so great that no single male was ever afforded an opportunity to mate alone.

A bright female steelhead begins to excavate her redd, which is distinguished by the circular patch of lighter colored gravel that were overturned while she was digging.

Spawning male winter steelhead rising after chasing several other males during tense competition for a female. The steelhead presumably gulped air to fill his air bladder, something that helps regulate vertical positioning in the water column.

Male steelhead with red-stripe and fungus courts the female while a smaller male resident rainbow trout holds in a satellite position prior to sneaking fertilizations.

I returned to the same place a few days later with my underwater video camera. After an hour of observation, I noticed one very small trout dart underneath the males and the female and retreat immediately after the eggs and sperm were released. I had previously observed male rainbow trout of 10-18 inches mating with female steelhead, but this trout was much smaller. Before I could identify the small fish, the female began to release eggs for a second time, and I noticed two more trout dart beneath her. This activity continued over the next few hours. After reviewing the tapes I identified the small fish as mature resident male trout, as evidenced by their release of sperm, no longer than seven inches. I did not see the little mature males eating eggs or insects entrained by the female's digging. As far as I could tell, they were only interested in mating. I was ecstatic with the find.

I have since found mature resident males with steelhead in other streams. Like repeat spawning steelhead, they are probably present to varying degrees in all populations. Indeed, resident males commonly cohabit with anadromous males in several species of salmon, trout, and char, so it should be no surprise that I found them mating with steelhead. Such males are especially common in Atlantic salmon, a species that shares similarities with steelhead. In Atlantic salmon, resident males can sire many offspring with larger anadromous females – including all offspring in some cases. Recent studies on steelhead populations in Washington and Oregon also suggest that resident males may father a large proportion of steelhead offspring (greater than 50%) in some years. Additionally, research on the Hood River, Oregon found that up to 40% of the steelhead genes came from resident rainbow trout. The thought of a seven-inch-long mature male friskily courting a 20-pound female was enough for me to reconsider the common dogma that 'big' males are the key to reproductive success.

A small mature rainbow trout rests below a redd, exhausted from trying to sneak fertilizations with a female steelhead.

Steelhead eggs are in various stages of development in spring, here within the same redd is an eyed egg and a juvenile emerging tail first. This range of development found in a single redd is one reason steelhead display such diverse life histories.

A steelhead spawning tributary cuts through a stand of alder trees brimming with fresh spring growth.

It is not only that resident males may mate with large anadromous females, but that the population complex of the two life histories is intertwined. My research found – including angling data, behavioral observations, and snorkel data – that resident rainbow trout are male biased (~ 70%) while steelhead are female biased (~ 58 %). This is consistent with male-biased resident rainbow and female-biased steelhead found in the rivers draining the Kamchatka Peninsula, Russia. Steelhead populations in the interior Columbia River are also often female dominant (up to 70% female), but little is known about resident trout sex ratios. Similar patterns exist in other salmonids. The reasoning is that larger size is critical to female spawning success because they carry more eggs and dig deeper nests – so they mostly migrate to the ocean. In contrast, small males can 'sneak' fertilizations with or without going to sea. Fish life histories are based on traits for successful perpetuation.

Sustaining steelhead into the future will require conserving their full suite of life history strategies – including resident forms in rainbow/steelhead populations. If research continues to find that resident males are as important to the productivity and diversity of steelhead as they are in Atlantic salmon, then a fish can't be judged solely by size. This does not mean the anadromous life history is any less important. It implies that all sizes, behaviors, and life histories are the rainbow/steelhead strategy for effective perpetuation in variable environments.

June

A Solstice Song to Trout

*Mayfly dries its wings in the morning sun
amongst the water beads that remained on the
hood of my truck after an early summer rainfall.*

The Elwha River at the mouth of the Grand Canyon flows full and blue from June snowmelt.

orn in June, my first fly-fishing casts came around my third birthday with a resulting doorway into nature. My earliest angling memories are of June fish, which include wild coastal cutthroat from small creeks in the upper Washougal River and redside rainbow trout in the Deschutes River. Those June days were warm, long, and full of opportunity. In addition to fishing, there were birds to observe and identify, rocks to turn over, insects and crayfish to capture, juvenile trout to chase in the shallows, and like many young boys, a variety of experiments performed with ant holes. The month was a biological Garden of Eden for a budding angler and naturalist. Accordingly, while June denotes the middle of the year, it is where my calendar of trout and rivers begins.

A large-spotted mature male redside rainbow trout from the Deschutes River, where I caught my first big trout and a river that our family has fished since the early 1900's. The Deschutes was my childhood playground and to this day remains my favorite trout river.

A mottled mayfly nymph rests in a small pool, this genus Ameletus is quite a strong swimmer in the open water and was found in the headwaters of a small tributary draining the Elwha River.

A coastal rainbow trout, short and plump, has more and smaller spots relative to its Deschutes counterpart.

My adult associations with June are largely drawn from those formative childhood experiences, although fishing the coastal rivers is now preferred to the inland Deschutes favored in childhood. Consequently, I delineate my memories of June into two eras – early years on the Deschutes River and my adult years on the coastal rivers of Washington and Oregon. The biological symbols of the two eras are the redside rainbow and the coastal cutthroat, respectively.

In childhood, my family spent one to two weeks camping each June at Trout Creek on the Deschutes before its continuous bustle of campers, guides, hikers, bikers, and rafters. Due to the lack of people, I, as a precocious hellion, proclaimed reign over most of the angling territory near our camp. My gear consisted of a six-weight fly rod, a box of Elk Hair Caddis and stoneflies, a tin of Mucilin, a few soft hackles, some water and Capri-Sun juice. I patrolled a mile of river from the mouth of Trout Creek upstream through the campground and onto the old railroad trail, occasionally expanding the territory as angling conditions dictated. I was short and scrawny, which helped me navigate the brushy banks where I pursued large Deschutes "redsides"

A uniquely spotted cutthroat that had been feeding on steelhead
fry in less than a foot of water near the river bank.

hunkered beneath overhanging alder limbs. During interludes I studied the behavior of a favorite bird, the Bullocks oriole, with hot breezy afternoons spent in the shade of alders watching them tend to their hanging nests. On other occasions, I honed particular angling skills, such as roll casting a bushy stonefly into the sharp mid-day wind. Those memories of adolescent freedom and opportunity remain incomparable.

I now fish the Deschutes once every year or two, in search of stoneflies, trout, solace and serendipity. However, each time I leave the river on one of its winding and dusty roads I wonder if it will be my final trip to that desert oasis of trout. Every year it is more difficult to accept the crowding and competition. While I may stop fishing the Deschutes, its redside rainbows have resulted in a lifelong influence. They inspired my more recent interests in coastal cutthroat. Coloration and spotting patterns of Deschutes redsides are remarkably diverse, especially in June when the trout are beaming in preparation for spawning. Such diversity initially eluded my notice in the cutthroat of my home river, the Washougal, largely because most of the cutthroat behind my house were hatchery-origin clones.

Stonefly nymphs — such as this individual with striking patterns on its back — are one of the primary food sources for trout.

I have since found great diversity in the appearance of native coastal cutthroat in the rivers of the Washington and Oregon coast. The morphological variation is so enthralling that I have spent thousands of hours angling for, photographing, observing, and enumerating coastal cutthroat. Cutthroat trout, including its several subspecies, are the "indigenous" *Oncorhynchus* of the northwest watersheds with an impressive breadth of life histories. Along the rainforest coast of Oregon and Washington, the coastal cutthroat subspecies inhabits a narrow belt of relatively short, steep rivers sculpted and recreated by glaciations, volcanism, and shifting sea levels. Here, the trout have survived, perished, and flourished under the strong selection of chaotic winter floods, parched summers, and the biological invasion of more recently evolved *Oncorhynchus* competitors. The reaction to these selective pressures is partly reflected in their aesthetic variability, an aspect of coastal cutthroat that I find especially prominent in June.

The variability in appearance of cutthroat is largely founded in life history strategy, with fish being either resident or anadromous. The resident fish grow, mature, and spawn in freshwater, with some individuals completing their entire life cycle within a few hundred meters of their

Thousands of mayflies litter the river's surface like confetti after New Year's.

birth place while others migrate within a watershed to feed and spawn. Anadromous individuals migrate to the ocean for a relatively brief period before returning to spawn in freshwater. The residents tend to be colored in hues of yellow, gold, orange, green and even violet which is sharply contrasted by relatively few large black opaque spots. The anadromous form is often pepper-spotted with amber backs and males' sides shaded pink at maturation; or pure silver tinged in blue with spots more faded if recently from the ocean environment. These patterns are basic generalizations. Some individuals may mature as residents and then become anadromous, or vice-versa, so spotting pattern is not necessarily a predictor of life history. Nonetheless, the general assumptions provide a starting point for comparing morphological variation.

In addition to life history, cutthroat appearance is also influenced by state of maturity. During June, the differences in appearance can be exacerbated by overlapping presence of pre- and post-spawn individuals. This is especially true in the larger mainstem rivers where individuals with

*Two coastal cutthroat trout synchronized in movement as they
ride the current in the headwaters of the Sol Duc River.*

differing life histories in various states of maturity commingle as they move up and down the river corridor in response to the mating season, typically ending around the end of June in the coastal rivers I frequent. Pre-spawn individuals moving upstream are plump and vividly colored while post-spawn individuals moving downstream to feed in mainstem rivers or the ocean have sunken bellies and muted coloring.

Ironically, my initiation into the diverse appearances of cutthroat in relation to life history and state of maturity occurred on a sunny June afternoon on my 28th birthday. During two hours in a single pool I landed three pre-spawn females with backs bathed in bronze, two post-spawn females with anal fins tipped in fungus, a large resident male gilded in gold and blackberry spots, and a handful of smaller silver and pepper-flaked fish that were apparently immature. That night I slept with the deep sleep of discovery and awoke the next morning refreshed with curiosity. The experience confirmed my growing belief – much like an answered

A stream in the headwaters of the Willamette River where rainbow and cutthroat trout are still present, but bull trout are now thought to be extinct.

prayer to a person of faith – that the underwater world of fish shrouded secrets scripted in the prehistoric prose of evolution: morphology.

For much of the year, the type of variation I experienced that day is not easily accessible to anglers. During winter cutthroat are also diverse in appearance. However, the colors and spotting can be drab due to turbidity and most fish are either in tributaries, which are often closed to angling, or are holding near bottom in the larger mainstem rivers, where they are difficult to catch. From mid-summer through fall, many tributaries are open to fishing and mainstem river conditions are adequate but the various life histories are widely distributed throughout the watershed. Consequently, an angler wishing to encounter a broad range of

Juvenile steelhead – the future of the famed Olympic Peninsula winter steelhead – spend most of their time foraging in June because food is abundant and water temperatures are neither too warm nor too cold.

diversity must cover an extensive watershed area. On the other hand, the relatively high flows, clear water, increasing temperatures, and ample food sources of June provide a narrow window in which an angler can fish a single run or reach of river and expect to encounter cutthroat in striking arrays of colors and spots.

It seems appropriate that the nexus of my birth month, favorable angling conditions, and biological diversity has fostered my adult interest in nature and fish through angling. The Deschutes and the rainforest rivers have served as mentors, transporting my curiosity down a sinuous journey of intrigue born during the solstice transition from spring to summer. Thus, the month in which I began life is the month I celebrate the native trout of the Pacific Northwest.

Coquihalla River canyon, lower Fraser basin in British Columbia, where historic wild summer steelhead numbers have been greatly depleted due to pipeline and highway construction.

Grand Ronde canyon in Oregon where wild summer-run steelhead used to return in July but are now delayed by dams, disorientation from barging as outmigrating smolts, and are a fraction of their former numbers due to hatchery-fish interactions at multiple life-history stages.

July

Canyon Steelhead and Headwater Trout

There are rivers that have carved canyons with deep pools kept in shadow for long summer hours that favor summer-run steelhead. The combination of deep pools and shorter hours of direct sunlight result in water temperatures at the bottom of these pools cool enough to allow steelhead to remain there for the warmest and driest periods of the year from June through September, and bedrock/boulder structure provides cover from flood and predator. Such pools provide secure refuges for up to 10-11 months until dispersal to spawning destinations from late January to May of the following year.

*Site of former Hemlock Dam removed from Trout Creek in 2009 to increase
wild-steelhead spawning and rearing habitat for Wind River.*

Wind River enters the Columbia River 155 miles from the Pacific. Before Bonneville
Dam inundated its lower mile, it had large returns of fall Chinook, coho, and chum salmon to a
lower two-mile reach now half gone, as well as good returns of winter-run steelhead and sea-run
cutthroat trout. However, at the two mile point Shepard Falls historically blocked access to the
30 miles of river upstream to all but quite a remarkable stock of steelhead – large individual size
for coastal summer-run populations, commonly 10-12 pounds with some to 20 pounds. While the
Rogue and Umpqua rivers of Oregon were of angling fame by the early 20th century for summer-
run steelhead of smaller average size, Wind River's steelhead were of more localized renown from
Portland through the Columbia Gorge. The only early writer to portray its steelhead was Enos
Bradner, a Seattle newspaperman, and by the time his book *Northwest Angling* was published in
1950, Wind River steelhead were already en route to great decline.

Ignorance is bliss. When I began reading *Northwest Angling* in the Camas, Washington
public library as a 5th grader in the mid 1950s I only knew that Wind River was within 25
miles of my home and one day I would fish for steelhead that overcame what may be singularly
the most difficult barrier anadromous fish anywhere overcome – Shepard Falls – historically

Wind River wild steelhead recovery is beginning with elimination of hatchery smolt releases in 1998.

a 43-foot drop in consecutive leaps of 5, 13, 13, and 12 feet. The falls limited access to only those steelhead that were at the peak of leaping athleticism the species is capable of. The upstream payoff was spawning grounds with sufficient gravel measured in the 1930s to support about 12,000 steelhead. This was decades after Wind River splash dam operations had created continuous floods of logs to awaiting sawmills leaving a denuded canyon, scoured river bed, and reduced productivity.

Wind River's original steelhead abundance is now unknown, but 15,000 at the time of Lewis and Clark's passing its mouth is in the ballpark. In 1951, 2,500 steelhead were estimated to have escaped to spawn after a sport catch of 500-1,000 – 3,000-3,500 total. By the time my father first took me to Wind River in 1957, a fish-way had been completed around the falls the previous year. Only 550-600 steelhead were estimated to have passed upstream in 1957. Its steelhead population was in rapid decline. Despite the falling numbers, I was to hook my first steelhead on a fly in the summer of 1961 in Wind River Canyon. The thrill of 16-year-old emotions fired by the canyon and that steelhead haunted me and eventually led to a life lived on rivers and conservation activism. In 1983, I would initiate the first snorkel surveys of Wind River

Shepard Falls on Wind River is altered with a fishway allowing hatchery Chinook upstream with reduced ability for wild summer steelhead to regain former abundance.

documenting the severity of wild-steelhead decline by that time. Only four steelhead were counted in four miles of river surveyed in the heart of the historic over-summering steelhead habitat where but 20 years before I had sighted nearly 100 in a single pool.

However, recovery efforts since that time for Wind River's wild steelhead have had gradual positive results. Elimination of hatchery steelhead releases, a long period of closure to steelhead fishing, habitat recovery efforts, elimination of straying hatchery steelhead at the Shepard Falls fish-way, and catch-and-release of all wild steelhead when angling is allowed have resulted in returns estimated at 1,000-1,500 wild summer-run steelhead in the better return years. And in 2009, a dam was removed that hindered steelhead entry into a major spawning tributary, Trout Creek. Within hours the first wild summer-run steelhead was sighted darting through the newly opened lake bed channel. Although Wind River remains far from its historic wild-steelhead productivity, from near sleep it has begun to awaken.

Further inland, the Grande Ronde River enters the Snake River 500 miles from the Pacific. From the outlet of the La Grande Valley it serpentines through an arid canyon for 95 miles beneath the towering grandeur of layered basalt whose formations often resemble nature's versions of medieval cathedrals magnified many-fold. Red in spring, brown in summer, black in winter, the colors of the basalt canyon alter... rock that seemingly transforms light into its own chemistry.

Upper Skagit River rainbow trout in British Columbia is now isolated by downstream dams in Washington.

The canyon is a cold place in winter, the river commonly encased in ice, and a hot place in summer, the encompassing rock walls a reflector oven. The payoff was historically beyond the canyon for salmon and steelhead – great expanses of high-valley spawning grounds on the Wenaha, Wallowa, and upper Grande Ronde rivers, and that above Joseph Creek's canyon.

Historically one of the most prolific producers of salmon/steelhead in the Columbia basin, the Grande Ronde minimally had hundreds of thousands. Although great runs of spring Chinook once ran through the canyon sections quickly to reach high valley gravel beds for August-September spawning, and long extinct sockeye ran to the sanctuary of Wallowa Lake, the memory of older fishermen of the 1940s and 1950s indicates considerable numbers of steelhead were already holding in upper canyon reaches of the Grande Ronde by July. With spawning in February at earliest and lasting to early June, steelhead had a long wait. Those destined for the upper valleys needed the cover of deep pools to overwinter in safety from ice and to provide cool water temperatures in summer at their bottoms along with spring seeps. The canyon areas that provide such characteristics are in proximity to upper valley spawning grounds whether on the mainstem or tributaries.

Today steelhead returning to the Grande Ronde are delayed by passage through eight Columbia/Snake River dams. Many are further confused after being collected and barged

Rattlesnake Grade winds down from Anatone, Washington into the Grande Ronde River canyon.

Stonecrop flower in Wind River canyon.

Rattlesnake in logjam on Icicle Creek of Wenatchee River basin Washington, a common inhabitant of interior river canyons that sometimes swims in rivers and may feed on juvenile salmon.

over 200 miles downstream as juveniles to circumvent losses at the dams with resulting loss of orientation on adult return making spawning destinations difficult to find. As a result, steelhead do not now typically reach cooler canyon waters of the Grande Ronde, Wenaha, Wallowa, and Joseph Creek until late October and November, many even later if at all. Instead they wander the increasingly warm waters of the Columbia basin using up vital fat and energy with consequences as yet little determined.

Some species of anadromous salmonids also include resident forms that can be isolated from the ocean by geologic or climatic events for as long as the population exists. Steelhead, cutthroat, Dolly Varden, bull trout, sockeye salmon, and Asian masu salmon all have resident forms. But it is now known that just as anadromous forms have given rise to many, if not all, of these resident forms, the reverse can also occur.

Populations of rainbow trout now isolated in cool streams in the mountains of Mexico once had anadromous passage before the great warming after the Ice Age disconnected the necessary threads of cold water to the sea. Similar populations of "resident" rainbow trout in the headwaters of some southern California streams disconnected from the Pacific by a decade of drought have responded to weather shifts back to more rainfall with magical returns of steelhead.

Cutthroat Creek: headwater stream of Methow basin in North Cascade Mountains of Washington.

Westslope cutthroat are inland residents but often share habitat with anadromous salmonids (Cutthroat Creek, Washington).

Green drake mayfly along Finney Creek of Skagit basin in Washington.

As disheartening as prospects for anadromous fish may now seem, these fish have survived glaciation and volcanism through quite remarkable adaptive traits, one of which is the ability to shift back and forth between residency and anadromy for some species or populations. Mexican trout have been naturally archived in the mountains where the migratory characteristics remaining in their DNA may activate 10,000 years from now with a return to global cooling – "voilà," now you see it, now you don't ... steelhead. Today there are many such populations presently disconnected above dams – including the vast region of the upper Columbia. Yet, take the dams out and they will return without any other aid, just as they did through much of their range after ice dams broke. These are creatures that know the ropes of survival selected by tens of thousands of years of adversity.

The broad, silent expanse of Kamchatka Peninsula where scientists have been studying char and steelhead with specimens collected by angling – Kvachina River in 1995.

August

Evolving Char and Increasing Pink Salmon

Are there examples of evolution in process? Indeed there are. One of these is thought to be in Asia where native char populations display wide differences.

The native char of western North America are of three species: Dolly Varden, bull trout, and Arctic char. The Asian side of the North Pacific has Dolly Varden, white-spotted char, yellowmouth char, and smallmouth char, as well as a number of very different morphological variations that Russian scientists indicate are in the process of speciation in northern Russia. In other words, as with the finches of the Galapagos Islands, northern Asia is a region where evolution is in active process – two differing regions of the world where birds and fishes are adapting to shifting environments.

Immense old growth like this cedar tree on Washington's Sauk River once blanketed the lowlands and river valleys of the eastern North Pacific Coast – the forest benefitting from nutrients of salmon carcasses dispersed by wildlife and the forest providing stable habitats for salmon.

Dolly Varden/Kundja hybrid (top), Kundja (bottom):
hybridization can be a means of new speciation.

The Cascade River of Washington's Skagit basin remains vital bull trout domain thanks to national park and wilderness headwaters.

In the state of Washington, for many years it was considered that bull trout inhabited primarily the inland region and Dolly Varden the coastal region. In fact, until the latter 1980s, bull trout and Dolly Varden were considered mere regional variations of the same species now broken out as two. Nevertheless, the two remain difficult to differentiate in the field. It was also once thought that Dolly Varden were commonly anadromous in Washington while bull trout were limited to stream residency or to lakes. This has also proven false. In Washington, bull trout are the more common Westside form that becomes anadromous while the few remaining Dolly Varden populations have proven to be resident. In a word, Pacific char are *confusing*. The science related to them will likely continue to alter for some time — as in fact, science continuously does, but not always with such rapidity as with char.

Whichever way the science may alter, the Pacific char are stunning fish as they approach their autumn spawning times. I like to follow the sea-run bull trout up into their spawning destination tributary areas of the Skagit River in the month of August. On initial spawning-run entry from late June into July their backs are gray with faint lemon spots and silvery sides sparsely

Mature female bull trout from cold-flowing Sauk River of Skagit basin in Washington.

Mature male bull trout from pristine Nass River basin in British Columbia.

The glacial outflow from the Sauk River provides sustained cold-water habitat in the Skagit basin for char but wild salmon are a fraction of former numbers that char and many other species depend on.

The lower Skagit River in Washington was once home to multitudes of char that went up tributary streams before it was altered by 150 years of settlement activities that cleared the former old-growth forests and reduced the returns of salmon.

speckled with pale crimson dots. But by August, after migrations of 90-125 miles to spawning destinations, the backs turn green to olive, the spots all stand out prominently whether yellow or brilliant red, and the lower sides take on the color of sunset. From mid September to spawning time in October, the colors increasingly darken – some turning a muddy brown. The heads of the males become long and angry. It is August when they are at a colorful perfection peak.

During the American/British boundary surveys between Canada and the U.S. in 1857-1859 naturalist John Keast Lord described vast autumn runs of char running up all the streams, large and small, of Puget Sound, the lower Fraser River and Vancouver Island. Along the smaller streams temporary tribal lodges lined the banks where young and old caught them in joyful celebration of their great abundance. They used hook and line baited with salmon roe or belly strips from trout, or by trapping them in baskets at rock weirs. Great numbers were split and dried, packed in bales, and provided a main winter store.

It is unknown today if these vast returns of char were bull trout or Dolly Varden. Char of 1-3 pounds, as then described, now rarely return to smaller streams anywhere in this same range. All U.S. bull trout have been listed as Threatened under the Endangered Species Act, yet Dolly Varden in the Lower 48 are likely far more depleted. Much misunderstanding continues. What is known is that all Pacific char are particularly dependent on very cold water, and those char in the anadromous zones are particularly dependent on the abundance of returning salmon as a food source (for carcass flesh, eggs, and fry). With logging, agriculture, and urban development,

Skagit River male pink salmon on fresh August entry.

water temperatures have increased over broad areas of their former North American range beyond their tolerances for productivity, and salmon runs now commonly five to 10 percent of former abundance (or already extinct) have left greatly depleted food sources.

The present widespread depletion of char in British Columbia and the Lower 48 are indicators of stream systems going to sleep. Yet, with remaining cold water and salmon abundant, the char of Alaska, Siberia, and Kamchatka remain in numbers not unlike those described in Puget Sound by Lord in the mid 1800s.

The Skagit is the one remaining system in Washington State with relatively large numbers of bull trout. Bull trout are nomadic and apparently do not home as specifically to the same stream, or river basin, as do most salmon. This means that relatively good numbers maintained by the Skagit basin could result in their spread to other streams if conducive water temperatures and numbers of salmon become more widespread through recovery efforts. In this regard, the Skagit basin is the "queen bee" of Puget Sound. The majority of all the glaciers in the Lower 48 are in the North Cascades the Skagit drains. Combined with less development than in other Puget Sound river basins, the Skagit continues to have cold water, more salmon, and therefore more bull trout than the others.

Tributary entry to Fraser River in British Columbia: pink salmon to the upper Fraser were eradicated by Hells Gate slide after 1913, but when passage was later provided they naturally recolonized mostly by natural means and now number in low millions in some parts of the upper basin in better years.

August is also the month when pink (or humpback) salmon begin returns to the Skagit and other Puget Sound river basins. In this part of their range most pink salmon return only on odd numbered years. Nevertheless, they were historically the most abundant of all salmon that returned to Puget Sound. However, they are small, averaging 2-4 pounds each, and have soft, light-colored flesh. These characteristics make them less preferred commercially in North America, but because they return at the same time as more targeted species they were incidentally caught in immense numbers and often discarded as waste in the late 1800s and early 1900s, leading to great depletions. Extensive arrays of trap nets owned by canneries that once lined Puget Sound particularly intercepted pink salmon, ten thousand or more sometimes caught in a single trapping.

However, after trap nets were outlawed in 1935 pink salmon returns began to rebound. In 2009, the Skagit River had what may have been the greatest return since the 1960s with about one million pinks entering the basin. As many as this may seem, Siberian biologist Mikhail Skopets indicates the Bolshaya River of Kamchatka (a river of similar size to the Skagit) has returns of 10-11 million pinks in the better return years.

Nevertheless, the Skagit pink return in 2009 was sufficient to provide a noticeable ecosystem response. Skagit bull trout numbers, depleted by autumn floods of great magnitude in 2003

These sockeye salmon returned to the upper Baker River of the Skagit basin – the only instance where trucking salmon above a dam has worked in the long-term. Sockeye are predominant in areas of Alaska and the upper Skeena and Fraser basins of British Columbia. In 2010, 25 million sockeye unexpectedly returned to the latter demonstrating that salmon abundance still remains possible with wakeful rivers.

and 2006, responded with a sudden large influx of bull trout in the winter and early spring of 2009/10. They were likely attracted out of Puget Sound and perhaps the Straits of Juan de Fuca and Georgia to take advantage of abundant eggs stirred up by winter freshets and February to April pink fry emergence. Did these same bull trout return to the Skagit in the summer of 2010 to spawn? Or were most of the bull trout wintering in the vicinity of larger Puget Sound temporarily drawn to the Skagit by the increased nutrients from pinks? Spawning surveys made in the Skagit basin in the fall of 2010 may provide answers.

It is known that throughout the North Pacific pink salmon have been steadily increasing for a couple of decades – perhaps a reverse response to global warming that is more negatively impacting other salmon species. In fact, both pink and chum salmon are apparently expanding their range northward as the Arctic increasingly opens. The news of global warming is not all bad – yet. What will occur as the Arctic becomes ice free remains little known. Past isolation of Atlantic from Pacific species may alter. What ocean current shifts may occur are unknown. But wild salmon have responded with survival in the past. Left to themselves, they will adapt as they did to the great warming of 7,000-8,000 years ago with temperatures warmer than any at present … *if* we get out of their way.

Kispiox River, British Columbia: wild-salmon abundance is the nutrient base for North Pacific riverine ecosystems in death as much as in life.

Indian Paintbrush: headwaters of Ahtanum Creek of Yakima basin in Washington where sufficiently cold flows continue to sustain resident bull trout and westslope cutthroat, but salmon are extinct due to passage eliminated by agricultural irrigation.

September

Time of Transition and Movement

A cased caddis crawling on river rocks before
it hatches and eventually becomes the big,
fluttering October caddis that is a favorite food
source of trout during late summer.

Three-month-old juvenile steelhead, only 2 inches in length, holding in shallow and warm water hoping to grow as fast as possible to survive the challenges of fall once the rainstorms arrive and the river flows peak.

September represents a climatic and biological transition from summer to fall. On the Olympic Peninsula, the seasonal shift is marked by shorter days, cooler temperatures, and brilliant sunsets. Mornings begin to feel like mornings, rather than a mere respite from summer's heat and humidity. Rain arrives in brief, but spirited squalls. Stream temperatures drop and flows rise and fall rapidly due to the antecedent moisture conditions. The changes in weather and stream flow bring new life into the river: the large adult salmon. There are other changes too; the deciduous trees begin to drop their leaves and some Chinook begin to perish after spawning. Because of this juxtaposition, September also carries – as Haig-Brown astutely observed – a "touch of death" in the air.

A pair of brown pelicans, which are common in September on the coast of the Olympic Peninsula, fly over the mouth of the Hoh River on a foggy morning.

The climatic shift of September invigorates the trout and steelhead that had grown stale during the warm and low stream flows of August. It also prompts the entry of fresh returning adult steelhead, cutthroat, coho, and Chinook into freshwater. The fish nose further upstream with each successive storm, their silvery luster of anadromy – like the season – gradually darkening over the course of the month. In the glacial rivers, char pay close attention to the salmon. After marauding spawning surf smelt on the coast, they follow the migratory salmon upstream to forage on eggs before moving into the headwaters to spawn later in the fall. The existing spring and summer Chinook intensify their spawning activity. They are in a hurry to finish before the monsoons of late fall wash their weak and decayed corpses into the floodplain. All adult stages of the salmon life cycle are present.

The plethora of fish movements ensures an angler rarely has the same experience twice. The pace of angling and observation is fast and provides little time for reflection. Metaphorically, September exudes the ambience of a subway terminal. There is the constant hustle and bustle of fresh anadromous fish passing through shallow riffles like turnstiles seeking a migratory corridor that will lead them to their final destination. Given the incredible diversity I find it impossible to identify a single species or subspecies as being representative. Instead, I celebrate the variable fall climate and the diversity of all salmonids.

Male Chinook salmon caught near tidewater after a bump in
flow triggered its upstream migration into fresh water.

September is partly a month of extremes and my life's activities have reflected that. In low-flow years I spend September snorkeling. Visibility is good and fish condense into smaller areas because less water is available, but they remain fairly active because water temperatures tend to be moderate. Juvenile salmon and trout forage intensively to put on size and fat before the onset of winter. Other juveniles gather in large schools near wood where they may seek refuge during colder and higher flows. Adult summer steelhead gather below waterfalls waiting to ascend during the fall freshets; and salmon school in pools, milling and rolling. There is no better month to consistently observe fish preparing for the onset of fall.

The conditions were so good during September of 2002 -- while working as a scientist for the Wild Salmon Center -- that I snorkeled 102 miles and only fished once. On some days I hid for several hours behind a rock or piece of wood, entranced by juvenile steelhead or coho competing for food or coastal cutthroat riding the currents like an eagle in the thermals. Other days I surveyed up to eight consecutive miles, often with James Starr, snorkeling through rapids and swimming through 600-yard-long pools. I was underwater for most of the month.

Low flows are not always easy in September though. It is not uncommon to shiver to exhaustion while trying to remain still in cold water. On 80°F days I may lose 10 pounds while

Low flows of the Calawah River canyon trimmed in bedrock and moss, five days later a flood barreled through the canyon and summer officially ended.

hiking fifteen miles in my wetsuit to access a remote stream. There is no grab and no screaming reel. The only glory is in enduring the challenge and, if lucky, perhaps observing something new.

In wet years, September more closely resembles October than August and snorkeling opportunities are greatly reduced and my time is more often spent angling. Early rainstorms soak the forest and storm winds blow multitudes of leaves into the rising rivers. Sometimes the conditions are severe enough to limit the effectiveness of my favorite tactic, the waking fly. Instead, I am forced to switch to the swung or twitched wet fly for coho and Chinook. While I do not enjoy the subsurface presentation as much, the fishing can be stellar because the high flows facilitate easy passage for fish.

Rather than wait for finicky fall rains, I sometimes migrate to Oregon's Blue Mountains where September is predictably stunning in early fall. A gentle breeze on a warm day spent along a stream surrounded by the changing shades of aspen and cottonwood is serene. The inland rainbow and cutthroat are even more diverse in appearance than the trout of the Olympic Peninsula. The favorable fall climate and beautiful trout are temptations to remain forever in the high desert of eastern Oregon. Nonetheless, I am always drawn back to the Peninsula and its unpredictable nature.

Fortunately, September's climate and stream flows frequently fall between the extremes, striking an amenable balance between the river and the fish. During the great years, three or four

A school of juvenile steelhead feeding on aquatic insects in a bouldery tailout.

pulses of rain hit the coast during the month. The weekly or bi-weekly rains regulate the upstream migration of new fish and redistribute the older fish with renewed vitality. Opportunities for angling are endless and I spend as much time on rivers as possible. Not forced into spatial extremes, I can fish anywhere and expect to catch any species with a Steelhead Caddis waked across the surface.

My favorite time is the first clear, foggy morning after a freshet. The first freshets often occur around Labor Day. I recall one particular morning fishing a moderate sized, non-glacial river. It rained just enough the previous three days to provide a splendid level of flow tinged with cedar-stain. In one run, I landed several coho and cutthroat, a steelhead, and lost a fairly large Chinook on a Steelhead Caddis. That day I hiked eleven miles drenched in sweat and waded over the tops of my waders twice to reach the other side of the river. Over the course of twelve years, a love for the life of rivers has been stirred by many Septembers. The rarity and transient nature of catching several species on the surface in one run is part of what makes the month so special.

Besides fish, there are the birds of my September memories on the Peninsula. Grouse are abundant with sudden thunderous flight amongst the river floodplain's young alder, willow, and snow berries. Cedar waxwings, robins, and varied thrush bobble around the tree tops stuffing themselves with the fermenting and intoxicating berries of mountain ash.

A female summer steelhead flares its fins—attempting to ward me off—as she stages in a bedrock pocket at the base of a series of waterfalls. She will later pass the falls to move upstream and spawn in late winter.

A small and curious juvenile Chinook takes a closer look into my camera.

Hundreds of juvenile Chinook and coho pack into a logjam in the Elwha River to feed and hide during the seasonal transition from summer to fall.

Brightly colored juvenile coho denoted by their black-and-white-tipped fins hold among algal-coated cobble. A closer look reveals a singular fish hiding under a rock in the middle of the photo, with its head and eyes barely visible. As fall approaches more fish will display this type of hiding behavior until winter, at which point nearly all juvenile salmon will become nocturnal.

A densely spotted and golden-yellow coastal cutthroat with a distended throat that resembles a boat keel, a feature unique to few despite offering advantages to capturing and consuming juvenile salmon.

My favorites are the brown pelicans that frequent the river mouths. I can watch for hours as the big birds take turns hovering above the water before diving into the ocean and returning with fish tails flopping from their beak.

Because September accounts for a seasonal shift I believe it is also an allegory for the beginning of one life and the end of another. The rise and fall of the river on a hydrograph chart closely resembles a cardiac cycle. Each pulse in river flow, like a heart beat, pumps new adult salmon into the rivers.

The orchestra of freshets and salmon movements breathes life into the previously stagnant landscape of summer and foreshadows the mortality of spring Chinook. In between pulses, the rivers drop and reveal their secrets. The salmon are in the river, but they feel exposed in the lower flows. They become nervous and grabby. An angler knows that such a window lasts only briefly, sometimes for as little as a few hours. Both angler and fish share some common instinct in feeling the climatic patterns. We become motivated by great anticipation. Each moment is fleeting. And so it is with September, a month represented by an increasing tension between rivers and salmon where climate sets the stage for the biological act of the mating season.

The N.F. John Day River meanders through the high-desert forest of eastern Oregon.

October

The Ice Travelers and Renewal of Vision

One of the few remaining places on the North Pacific Rim where a significant geographic area still exists with much of the wild salmonid "fabric" still intact is Russia's Kamchatka Peninsula. It provides an opportunity not unlike what Charles Darwin had in his voyage on the *H.M.S. Beagle* with arrival to the Galapagos Islands in 1835.

In late August of 1995, I left my residence in the Grande Ronde River Canyon and drove northward across the arid expanse of eastern Washington en route to Seattle. The next day I was to fly to Kamchatka as a member of a joint Russian/American scientific expedition to study steelhead populations there. In over 40 years of fishing for, living with, and studying steelhead, I thought I understood their past, their present, and a future that held little optimism for them. This was particularly so for upper Columbia/Snake basin steelhead of the Grande Ronde,

Big bend of the Klickitat River in Washington: considered in 1950 to have sufficient gravel to support 50,000-75,000 spring Chinook but today averages little more than 300 wild spring Chinook annually and with wild steelhead in great decline.

Russian/American science expedition to study Kamchatka Peninsula steelhead used angling to collect samples.

Kvachina River science expedition camp (river channel to left of tents):
winter begins in late October in Kamchatka where steelhead are known as The Ice Travelers.

First Nation totem at Kispiox Village, BC: occupied
village sites with evidence of salmon use date to
9,000 years ago in the Columbia River basin.

Finney Creek of the Skagit basin in Washington:
a large pink salmon return in 2011 attracted black
bears and will help provide sufficient fat for winter
denning and birthing of healthy cubs.

Large resident rainbow from Kamchatka's Utkholok River: Russian scientists have long noted that steelhead/rainbow spawn together and it is a means to maintain population stability over time.

Russian gillnet catch of The Ice Travelers from which samples and measurements were taken.

Snake, Clearwater, Wenatchee, Methow, Asotin Creek and those others where wild steelhead are clearly reeling from multiple effects – passage problems through eight or more dams the most well known, but ironically the most devastating being hatchery programs whose best intentions are instead eliminating them. The latter is apparent from wild-steelhead populations similarly reeling that are above only one or two Columbia dams (such as those of the Deschutes, Hood, Klickitat, and Wind rivers), or those above no dams at all (such as the Washougal and Kalama river, or even those of more distant Puget Sound).

    I had no notion of what to expect of Kamchatka – what it might teach me of steelhead, of human beings, and of myself. I only knew I needed to go there … take a last look at one of the remaining wild places. More important, as lovely as the two months of September and October might have been on the rivers of eastern Oregon and Washington, I needed to renew a mind laden with the poison of pessimism for these rivers' futures as viewed through the filter of disappearing wild steelhead.

Skeena River in British Columbia with eagle gliding into view continues to have excellent habitat but wild salmon and steelhead suffer from over exploitation in commercial fisheries related to harvest targeting sockeye returning to artificial spawning channels on tributaries to Babine Lake.

Steelhead drying at native Koriak camp, Kamchatka: wild salmon abundantly sustained North Pacific Rim aboriginal people for 7,500 years.

Talons of dead bald eagle at O'Toole Creek of Skagit River where the largest over-wintering eagle population in the Lower 48 depends on salmon carcasses.

*Male chum salmon carcass freshly spawned on the
Skagit River where they spawn from late October to early
January; post-spawned bull trout recover eating their eggs and
flesh and the carcasses feed over-wintering bald eagles.*

My experience of Kamchatka would be that of a vast and silent expanse where fishery discoveries might occur at any moment. New species of char were not only being recently discovered there, but a group of seemingly four differing trouts on the Sedanka River were proving difficult to describe as either rainbow or cutthroat. During nights at the remote Kamchatka camps there were even science discussions that northeast Asia is potentially where evolution of both species began as the Pacific trouts. In fact, the remaining richness of fishes with evolutionary ancient lineages in the region has suggested to me that it was an epicenter for salmonid evolution, potentially supporting intermediary species between Atlantic and Pacific trout, char, and salmon. The place set my mind spinning – not only with the sense of realizing how little is known, but with the understanding that pessimism is but a symptom of lack of seeing the larger whole of nature outside the temporal limitation of self-centeredness in an individual lifetime. In a word, I came to *bloom* with joy of discovery.

Kamchatka took me back to that time of first discovery in 1963 when my father and I rented a boat from an Indian at Lake Babine's Topley Landing. With complete trust in the rented motor, the 10-gallon gas can, and the instructions he provided, we reached the Babine River salmon counting weir some 65 miles distant via travel down two lakes and the river. It was at the Babine weir where my mind would be forever permeated by the what salmon abundance smells like – not so much the vision of pink salmon carcasses stacked three deep in a continuous line along the river's edge, but the overpowering odor that left me staggered by it in the first 24 hours of adjustment. For three days we were alone with that smell of abundance – just us, the bear tracks everywhere, and a young fish biologist who came each day to tally the salmon passage. But my innocence of that initial hope in the experience of Babine abundance in 1963 had gone dead for 30 years.

In those first two months in Kamchatka in 1995, my previous limitations of having tried to understand salmonids of the northwestern United States through the rivers and creeks of a country impacted by 150 years of aggressive resource exploitation became immediately clear. Kamchatka is a place where the filters of human uses that obscure the desire to understand are reduced, and where the scientific quest for essential truths is less inhibited by volumes of accumulated misinformation drawn from tattered resources. On return to Kamchatka for two more months in 1996, it was as if I had come home to a place of mind that was native to human existence … human mind before its psychic encounter with human proliferation through the turn to agriculture and sun clocks rather than moon and river clocks.

Methow River in eastern Washington where wild steelhead are threatened by hatchery steelhead. However, long – eradicated coho may be re-establishing through hatchery introductions as one of the few hatchery reintroduction successes that only time can better evaluate regarding their continued persistence or not if the hatchery releases were to be stopped.

In 1996, I was to remain right up until ice-up on the Kvachina River. This was to determine if steelhead actually initiate a large migration under the cover of ice as described by a Russian biologist three decades earlier. As is common with Russians, it led to a poetic name for steelhead – The Ice Travelers. By late October the ice came to Kamchatka with three feet of snow banked against the windward side of our red yurts – nothing but Siberian silence and snow horizon to horizon. As the river slushed over with the initial phase of the long winter's ice the Russians got in one last haul of the nets and up came a large catch of steelhead entering from the Sea of Okhotsk. With it came camp jubilation. The "myth" of The Ice Travelers was confirmed along with the continued legendary status of the earlier biologist. That biologist's son was a member of our tiny encampment on that snow bound expanse, he having followed in his father's footsteps.

The rivers of the Kamchatka Peninsula provide the intact example of what the "fabric" of the anadromous fish population complex once might have been in the northwestern United States. It's a fabric built on diversity, abundance and the beneficial interactions of varied fish species and stocks in their adaptations to differing habitat niches and to each other. Pacific salmon with overlapping return timings mutually create localized freshwater ecosystems built on their own maximized abundance perhaps because of, rather than in spite of, volcanic origin rivers carrying heavy silt loads in a region of continued active volcanism on the peninsula's mountain central spine.

O'Toole Creek of the Skagit River in Washington during first October freshet that will bring in pink salmon on odd years, coho and chum all years, and occasionally Chinook salmon. In the 1850s naturalist John Keast Lord described similar streams that could not contain all the salmon and some were forced out onto the banks.

Without experiencing Kamchatka rivers, it is difficult to convey the notion that volcanically "degraded" rivers may not be a limitation to anadromous fish abundance, but actually may have initiated an evolutionary process that has resulted in what might be termed "suspended" or "floating" self-creative ecosystems that are detached from, and minimally dependent upon, the innate productive qualities of volcanic origin rivers except for open access into them and cold, unpolluted, flowing water.

The lower sections of the three rivers near our camp consisted of long reaches of small gravel mixed with immense quantities of fine sediments. But the mounds of pink, chum, and Chinook salmon nests were everywhere testimony that mud-impacted gravel supported fish. Intensive spawning competition and repetitive construction of salmon nests on top of each other can actually create cleaner gravel for each succeeding spawner. Making volcanically impacted spawning gravel productive is virtually dependent upon sacrificial "inefficiency" through maximized competition on spawning grounds in the appearance of wasteful mayhem. Clean gravel appears secondary to the primary necessity of maximized salmon abundance in order to *create* the habitat required for their own self-sustaining success.

Kamchatka provides the example of how Pacific salmon have long dealt effectively with so-called "degraded" habitat through the mayhem of abundance and in subsequent mass martyrdom resulting in nutrient-rich streams and lakes for progeny. Abundance perpetuates abundance.

November

Death and Deserts

A pair of maple leaves on the Skagit River denoting the
onset of fall and its implications for spawning salmon.

A pair of Chinook salmon resting behind a boulder in a riffle as they take a break from the rigors of spawning. They will succumb to physical depletion and die within the week.

*A*s a child living on the banks of the Washougal River, November was the first month I began to associate death and emotion. Sometime around the age of six my father drove us to a favorite fishing hole where I had played and landed one of my first steelhead on a fly. The river pinched through a rapid at the bottom of a pool and descended into a long choppy run bounded on one side by bedrock and overhanging alder trees. The other side was flanked by a 100-yard-long slice of bouldery floodplain. The river spread across a broad gravel bar at the tailout – perfect for spawning salmon. I did not know why we took the trip, but I did know that November was the season of salmon.

A female steelhead with the unique coloration and spotting patterns – fewer and larger spots relative to coastal steelhead – of steelhead populations inhabiting the interior Columbia River.

We walked downstream to a lone patch of grassy meadow. In the shallow tailout several large salmon were splashing and chasing, which piqued my attention. There, in an increasing drizzle that forebode the arrival of a powerful fall storm, my father told me the story of spawning salmon. He explained that juveniles outmigrate to the ocean in spring after rearing in freshwater for a period ranging from months to years. A year or more later they return to their natal stream as adults to mate. Females will seek out and fight for areas where they dig their nests, guarding precious eggs until the life force disappears. Males will wage war and sacrifice their bodies for the right of first choice in females. Once the nesting areas have been sorted amongst females and male dominance levels established, the spawning of the next generation's offspring commences. I listened as the salmon visibly carried out their final days.

My father's story and the violent salmon behavior were enthralling and formative. I recall his hands moving eloquently, pointing out the differences between coho and Chinook. His voice was sure and clear. I, as a wee lad, admired him for the riverside lessons. My fresh emotional pallet and young mind instantly craved a similar knowledge of rivers and fish. I wanted to be an extension of my father and family, and pledged from then on that I would forever love rivers and fish. My emotional bearings were formally established in that day's lecture.

The long head and thick lower jaw of this inland male steelhead contrasts against the smaller, blunt head of his female counterpart.

Two or three weeks later we returned to the same location. My emotions ran high with excitement and I must have been a pain in the ass for my father. On arrival, though, I instantly sensed a different ambience from the previous visit. The river had risen substantially and was the color of hot cocoa. The alder and maple trees had lost the majority of their leaves. The splashing and fighting salmon were gone.

I asked my father: What happened to the salmon? He pointed to a jumble of drift wood and sand. Jutting up was a blackened head with a snarled jaw and eyeless sockets providing a view into the skull. A spine, worn fins, chunks of white flesh, and rotted skin were all that remained of the body. I investigated more closely, a miniature Sherlock Holmes noting clues. There were other carcasses. The smell was putrid. The sandy beach surface was scuttled with paw prints, bird tracks, and carcass bits. My father noticed me hunched over the sand in thought and mentioned that black bear, otter, eagle, skunk, raccoon or one of many other animals savaged most of the tasty parts. A mental door opened for me: death was final and real.

The memories after that are vague but the emotions are not. My father confirmed that all the salmon died. I became flush with a sick stomach. I wanted to cry and puke. The beautiful fish were dead. I had smelled the rotting fish before. I had poked and prodded their carcasses with sticks.

A steelhead river winds a blue ribbon through an otherwise nondescript and desolate brown landscape, offering water and its gift of life to the riparian zone.

I had investigated. But never before had I felt overwhelmed by hopeless melancholy. It was the first time I remembered feeling grave depression. So strong was the emotion in my heart that not until my mother passed away in my early 30's did I ever again feel a similar level of sorrow. To this day the rivers of the coast and lower Columbia in November evoke a sense of sickness and depression that I can only relate to that early childhood experience with the Washougal River's salmon.

Since childhood I have continued to watch salmon excavate nests, spawn and die. In fact, I now spend more time observing salmon in November than fishing for them. Although angling for coho and Chinook remains exciting, their freshwater adult life is so fleeting and their behavior so intriguing that the methods of underwater videography, photography and observation seem more relevant in this day and age of declining fish runs. Plus, the salmon season infects many anglers with "salmon fever", which inevitably triggers a "logging-road culture" of poaching, beer, and guns. To avoid the anglers and sharpen my observation skills I seek those small tributaries with spawning salmon that are closed to fishing. There I try to rekindle those raw and virgin emotions experienced during the childhood trips with my father.

While I love November in the rainforest, each year there comes weariness with salmon death and a growing uneasiness with the approaching winter's darkness. To mitigate, I often migrate to the tributaries of the interior Columbia River to fish for desert steelhead and soak in the warmth of the waning fall sun. While water temperatures may decrease sharply in the interior rivers, their flows remain relatively low and stable. This contrasts with coastal rivers riding a hydrologic roller coaster during the onset of the flood season. Plus, the hardy strain of small inland steelhead are wiry risk-takers that continue to rise to a surface fly in relatively cold water temperatures.

November is when the beavers start working hard to fall trees for the onset of winter. Here a particularly ambitious beaver has a long haul left to finish a large alder tree.

There are two types of beavers on the Olympic Peninsula, this is the rarely seen and feisty mountain beaver — only about 12 inches in height – that burrows its nests and tunnels into the soft soil of hillslopes and river banks.

Turning alder leaves make their last stand in late fall in a rugged canyon pool on the Elwha River, a river where two large dams are being removed in a large-scale attempt to recover the formerly abundant populations of salmon and steelhead.

A large and densely spotted coastal cutthroat trout holds in a shallow feeding lie next to shore during a particularly cold and dry November in 2002 that prevented the upstream migration of salmon across the Olympic Peninsula, but in turn, offered an extended angling season for these beautiful trout.

The November differences in climate and hydrology between the coast and the desert provide an invigorating juxtaposition. Salmon are spawning and dying on inland rivers too, but the steelhead are alive and fresh. They will remain in the rivers over the winter and spawn from mid-spring through early summer. Some steelhead have been in the rivers since July, but others may have just arrived. Those males that have been in the river for a couple of months begin to display their red lateral stripes and kiped jaws. Freshly arrived females still resemble polished silver, a faint gray torpedo that sprinted up the mainstem Columbia as though left behind by earlier arriving classmates. This variability in steelhead appearance is always a desert-river highlight.

A male coho decked out in his bright red spawning colors hides behind two female coho.

Coho spawning is often in full swing as November transitions to December.
Here a female coho prepares to excavate her redd while three males take
position and prepare to release their milt.

Salmon carcasses with eyes intact have not been dead for long. The eyes are a favorite treat of the birds. This ghostly Chinook gazes lifelessly into the sky, appearing to look for the eagles, crows, ravens, and gulls to consume its flesh and pass its nutrients on to the riparian ecosystem.

But the desert experience is more than angling, more all encompassing in view and spirit. The vast landscapes of plateaus and valleys offer striking visual insight into the geologic, hydrologic, and volcanic past of the interior Columbia. The scenery is always balanced by another sense – the scent of sage or the calls of valley quail and rambling chuckle of chukar. The game bird calls are often the first sound I hear as the mists rise off the rivers under the darkness of early morning. When the first sun rays warm my face there is little thought of leaving the desert.

On the coast November views are more intimate: shrouded by sharp mountain peaks, fog, and forests of spruce and hemlock. The birds have largely gone quiet, winter wrens occasional exceptions and chirping eagles fighting over fish guts. Mornings are virtual silence, thoughts only slightly broken

Fellow extreme fish biologist Ian Tattam casting his Spey rod on the John Day River where summer steelhead provide the last month of vibrant life before the landscape freezes over for winter.

by the sound of rushing water. It is with these rainforest rivers my soul remains attached. They are the rivers that bond my present experiences to those I had with my father as a child living on the Washougal, a once famous river on the verge of slipping into a human-induced slumber.

I will never replicate that moment with my father in a first understanding of both salmon and death. But ultimately, more than salmon death or desert steelhead, November remains the time for me to watch the salmon as the primary lesson. The passing of information through generations from father to son has been and remains a staple of the human culture. In my family's case, the river has always been the location of such lessons. And in many ways that is the goal of this book, to pay tribute to one of the fathers of conservation – Roderick Haig-Brown – and pass our observations of rivers and fish from one clan to the next.

December ice formation along the shoreline of Washington's
Skagit River as flows recede during the cold.

Winter snowfall on Washington's Skagit River.

December

Flood, Ice, Snow and Salmon and Steelhead at Glacier Toes

Coastal flooding commonly occurs in the months of November and December. If new snow in the Cascade and Olympic Mountains is followed by a storm system from the Central Pacific swept inland by balmy winds of 60° F and accompanying heavy rainfall, what is termed a "rain-on-snow" event is the inevitable result.

Finney Creek of Skagit basin, after snowfall (top) and during rain-on-snow event (bottom).

My first riverside experience of such an event was in 1972 on the Washougal River. Our 1920s house was built 15 feet from the river's edge and 15 feet above it. Awakened before dawn by a continuous roar outside the bedroom window, my flashlight shone on a five-foot-diameter log in a slow cartwheel lifting it to eye level as it whisked past at 15 mph – the usual chuckle of its friendly waters raged in a brown torrent. I grabbed wife and child, John six months old, and packed them into the old VW camper. As curiosity overcame panic we drove upstream to the bridge at Salmon Falls. A hundred feet downstream the river erupted from the canyon, its bottom

Deforest Creek landslide in the NF Stillaguamish basin, Washington occurred during a winter storm event in 1983 as a result of logging on State, private, and Federal forest lands; shown 27 years later it remains a massive surreal slash across the landscape from which salmon, steelhead, bull trout and human beings suffer long-term consequences.

boiling to the top with boulders the size of basketballs bouncing on the surface like rattling dice. I've since experienced eight major floods as penance for living on rivers the past 41 years.

As devastating as floods can be, if frequency is not high – say 20 years per major event – they also create the dynamics of new gravel recruitment for spawning and large trees ripped from banks for eventual channel stabilization in the form of logjams and protective fish habitat. However, due to elimination of forest cover on mountain slopes as well as valley floors, and due to global warming, frequency of major flood events keeps escalating. With resulting 5-10-year major flood frequencies there is little opportunity for stabilization to occur. Salmon are left to struggle in continuously shifting and modified habitat that their genetics and life histories are too slow to adapt to.

Yet, coho salmon depend on December storms of moderate magnitude to provide spawning entry to small creeks they specialize in with high productivity and which they share with sea-run cutthroat and steelhead in January, February, and even into March in some instances.

*Entry of these coho to Savage Creek of the Skagit River required
several high flows to breach the beaver dams downstream.*

December storms were also the historical time of winter-run steelhead entry on rivers from the Queen Charlotte Islands south to Mexico's Baja Peninsula. However, the run-timing of winter steelhead throughout western Washington has been dramatically altered by fisheries management since the beginning of the modern hatchery program in 1960. December through February wild steelhead, once the dominant return period in Washington, have been nearly eliminated in many rivers due to harvest targeted on early entry steelhead for several decades. Washington's steelhead managers – the Department of Fish and Wildlife and the Boldt case treaty tribes – claim that December through February steelhead harvest is limited to hatchery steelhead that has left wild steelhead protected. However, over 100 years of historic reports from federal, state, and tribal sources all indicate that 55-95% of historic wild winter steelhead in Washington returned from December to February. Only recently have the State's own sport harvest records back to 1947 and tribal harvest records back to 1934 been resurrected, and federal reports back to 1889. These indicate a steady trend of rivers that had tens of thousands of wild steelhead now down to hundreds, or a few thousand at most. This has resulted in the 2008 listing of Puget Sound steelhead under the Endangered Species Act as Threatened.

Washington has been largely left with late return steelhead from March through June that were historically the least numerous and least broadly adapted to the majority of Washington's

Extensive wetlands (top) and beaver dams and ponds (bottom) once covered much of the eastern Puget Sound lowlands of Washington creating essential rearing habitat for salmon and steelhead, as well as providing a buffer to hold back heavy rainfall and melting snow in winter and sustaining summer flows.

Visiting Russian biologist, Mikhail Skopets, with large, wild
early return Sauk River steelhead to be released.

once extensive and productive steelhead stream habitats. Until the natural early run-timing of wild winter steelhead that best fits Washington habitat characteristics is restored, there can be no recovery. The good news is early-run steelhead remain at remnant levels and are restorable over time, but only if the co-managers make hatchery and harvest decisions to prevent further driving them toward extinction. It is but one example where fish management itself is a primary driver of wild stock depletions.

December can also have periods of prolonged sub-freezing weather when streams locked in ice and snow expose a visually stunning face of nature left to those few who seek out, rather than avoid, the discomfort of cold. Buried in the gravel and cobble of the stream bottoms, or far back in woody debris, juvenile salmonids wait winter out – rarely venturing from their concealment until warmer flows increase their cold-blooded metabolism. Even in "normal" winter periods, they venture out to feed only at night until spring's gradual warming provides mobility levels to avoid daylight predators.

If subfreezing temperatures last a week or more, the water can drop to $32°$ F and still continue to flow except in areas near bottom where the lack of current initiates "anchor ice," a thick slush that gradually builds upward lifting the entire stream bed, sometimes 2-3 feet. At the same time the surface of the quiet water at the stream edges freezes. As the river recedes with lack of rain it leaves sometimes fantastic sculptures, and snow can muffle sound with a baffling silence.

*Receding Washougal River flow during December chill with the
former waterline archived in crystalline sculpture of ice.*

At a longer-term scale of hundreds of Decembers of accumulated snow and ice, resulting glaciers can fill former river valleys. Although glaciers can eliminate fish habitat as valleys fill with ice hundreds or thousands of feet thick, the melt at the toe of retreating glaciers is frequently first trapped as a lake by the gravel moraine pushed ahead of it before spilling over into a river. Salmon and steelhead populations have extended up and retreated back out of river valleys in a slow "do-si-do" with glaciers for thousands of years. Sockeye salmon have colonized glacial origin lakes as their adaptive specialization.

Alaska's Situk River has had a continual dance with glaciers that periodically blocked Russell Fjord near Yakutat until it fills as Russell Lake and spills over into the Situk River, transforming it from a creek-like stream of about 150 cfs to a great river of 20,000 cfs. Today the Situk is small and clear, but in the mid 1800s it was a glacial lake outflow, large and muddy. Twice in the past 25 years, Hubbard Glacier, the longest tide-water glacier in North America, has grown across Russell Fjord to create Russell Lake, but the ice did not hold, releasing the rising lake waters back into Yakutat Bay before it breached into the Situk. It is predicted the growing glacier will eventually seal it off and again transform the Situk.

In the meantime, the Situk is remarkably productive for such a small river with both river-spawning sockeye as well as more typical lake sockeye that return to Situk Lake. It is a low gradient river providing classic coho habitat, and it does have large runs of coho, but it also has strong runs of Chinook, pinks, and chum. What it does not look like is a highly productive

Geomorphologist, George Pess, examines ice at Harlequin Lake, Alaska, a glacial lake at head of the Dangerous River.

steelhead stream due to lack of cobble/boulder riffle habitat thought to be particularly associated with steelhead/rainbow productivity. Yet, in 1952, after nearly a decade of bounty money paid for dead steelhead and Dolly Varden by a local cannery in the 1930s as predators on salmon eggs and fry, they had recovered to the point that 25,000-30,000 steelhead kelts were passed downstream through a weir intended to primarily count returning sockeye salmon. Depleted again down to 1,000-1,500 steelhead from 1953 into the 1980s, recovery efforts have since resulted in as many as 15,000 steelhead in recent years.

By contrast, Washington's over 10-fold larger Skagit River, which as recently as the latter 1950s had run-sizes of 20,000-40,000 wild steelhead and about 100,000 in 1895, had a 2009 run-size of no more than 2,500 wild steelhead.

What the future might bring to the Situk River remains to be seen, but glacial lake overflow is imminent due to the anomaly of Hubbard Glacier's growth in this time of otherwise mostly shrinking glaciers. How salmon and steelhead respond will provide a 150-year glimpse back in time when the Situk was similarly a glacial river of great size in the dance of wild salmon with ice. The nearby Dangerous River's glacial toe at Harlequin Lake provides a contemporary view of what the Situk has been and will again be. Yet, the most productive area of the Situk between Situk Lake and the Old Situk glacial outflow channel may be little affected, with continued high salmon productivity, just as tributary streams provided continuing steelhead and coho productivity in the Toutle River after the boiling mudflows of the 1980 eruption of Mt. St. Helens.

Top: The Situk River in Alaska today is a small, productive salmon/steelhead stream.
Bottom: The Dangerous River in Alaska is similar to what the Situk River was and again may become.

A River Calendar's Future

*Black bear tracks on a sand bar after it had
been feeding on salmon carcasses, which further
supports the notion that no animal is more
synonymous with salmon than the bear.*

Whitefish hold in a cold-water plume behind a boulder in the S.F. Calawah River. They spend much of their day behind this particular boulder during warm summers when water temperatures are stressful, but during cool summers they spread out more evenly across the river because temperatures are not a problem.

Calendars provide humans with a means of communicating temporal associations and patterns that are culturally important. The temporal bearing of the earliest calendars, dating to 20,000 to 35,000 years ago, was woven around the fabric of lunar cycles, fish and animal migrations, and availability of other foods. That began to change 6,000-7,000 years ago when the Egyptians developed the 365 day solar calendar, which roughly followed the cultural transition from hunter/gatherers to agriculturists. Less dependent on lunar cycles that contribute to fish and animal migrations, each New Year was instead marked by the annual floods in the Nile River that Egyptians depended on for planting crops. Changing measures of time have thus reflected an altered course of human culture from worship of *Nature* to that of increasing manipulation of and disconnection from nature. Nonetheless, one constant among the variations of historic calendars is the importance of rivers as a place of sustenance and spirituality.

Large male Chinook salmon in the lower Elwha River holds in the pit of a redd awaiting the return of a female. This fish was probably 40 pounds and its offspring will return to a river free of dams for the first time in nearly 100 years.

My natural measure of time is that of the cyclic pattern of river life from year to year – a river calendar. Rivers are my life-blood. This comes from an infancy spent in a bedroom perched over the Washougal River with my developing mind permeated by its sounds night and day – from the gentle purr of drought in summer to the roar of winter flood carrying 150-foot-long trees swiftly past. It also comes from an adulthood spent on rivers. This path was strongly influenced by my father, his by his father and Roderick Haig-Brown. This book – from a father and son – is a memorial river calendar to Roderick Haig-Brown, a family's thoughts and images inspired by the lives of rivers, salmon and a great conservationist.

A theme throughout is that rivers and salmon of the Pacific Northwest have undergone great change. The rate and extent of change is striking if you compare the Campbell River and its salmon runs described in Roderick Haig-Brown's *A River Never Sleeps* to the Campbell River of today. Due to dam construction and other human pressures, the seasonal patterns in salmon migration and spawning currently represent only a fragment of what he described 65 years ago in his seminal river calendar. The Washougal River my father and I knew has also changed. The spring run of summer steelhead has largely disappeared, wild coho were replaced by hatchery returns, cutthroat exist only in reduced numbers and the once Spartan river banks are littered with homes. We mostly avoid the Washougal now. Only twenty years after leaving the Washougal our calendar is outdated, the river

As a little boy I spent many hot summer days chasing and catching crayfish in the Washougal River. This fellow flashed his pinchers from his hidy-hole, warning me of the consequences of further intrusion.

and its fish altered. Further human population increases and expansion are predicted to be extensive in the Pacific Northwest and those changes will be reflected in rivers and fish.

The simplest way to predict the condition of the rivers of tomorrow is to observe the rivers of today and reflect on the rivers of the past. The rivers my father and I have known, and those Roderick Haig-Brown knew, have been places of revelation for us as both anglers and biologists. It was angling that initially drew me to salmon and rivers, but snorkeling and observation have proven more enlightening. Angling at its best provides an emotional thrill of pursuit, but underwater experiences have been more magical for what is revealed.

The most memorable underwater moments have provided revelations across several scales of thought. One of these moments had to do with the most basic need of salmon. Cold flowing water is essential to salmon persistence. Although many factors influence salmon, the Pacific Northwest is a region where temperature has altered and will continue to alter their life histories. Both temperature and flow are the basis for migratory movements and are the foundation of any anadromous fish river's calendar. The Olympic Peninsula rivers that I have written of are often thought of as cold and flush with summer flow, but encroaching climate change and unsustainable land-use practices suggest an unpredictable future. As with calendars past, the relevance of our river calendar will depend on how much future value we humans place on the natural world.

A native female steelhead from the interior Columbia River where dams and land-use practices
have altered water temperature and flow regimes, which in turn have negatively impacted the entry
time and upstream migration of steelhead. Only time will tell if they are able to adapt quickly
enough to persist in the face of further human-induced alterations to their natal rivers.

The summer of 2002 I was working with James Starr, friend and fellow biologist, conducting snorkel surveys on Olympic Peninsula rivers. It was abnormally warm and dry. From mid-July through early August water temperatures in the upper Calawah River reached 73°-75°F during the day and cooled only to the mid-60s°F at night. The Sol Duc and Calawah rivers would later peak at 82°F in early September. Because the rivers were too warm to ethically fish for salmon or trout, I began snorkeling every evening and weekend targeting a two-mile stretch of river. Within the two-mile reach – which was always warmer than the rest of the river – there was one pool that during previous four summers supported a school of 25-45 mountain whitefish. But during 2002 the school consisted of only 10 fish. They were the only whitefish within a mile of river in either direction. They were a small and isolated group.

Several times while sitting on the shore, I noticed that the school was not only smaller, but they behaved differently. They hung directly on the river-bottom in three feet of water behind a large boulder directly in the middle of the pool. When I began to snorkel they became frightened and fled from the boulder, but after I left the fish always returned. In prior summers, the whitefish held mostly in deeper areas near the head of the pool. I wondered why their behavior had changed and why they displayed such high fidelity to a particular place.

A week into the surveys I stumbled onto the reason by accident. I forgot my wetsuit. Unprotected by neoprene, I walked behind the boulder that had attracted the whitefish. My toes instantly became cold. Below the surface there was a plume of colder water originating from the base of the boulder: a groundwater seep. Using a thermometer I snorkeled back and forth to estimate the area influenced by the seep. The colder plume was two feet wide by four feet long and extended a foot above the stream bottom. The entire pool was over 100 yards long and 30 yards wide. The spot behind the boulder was analogous to a pimple on the ass of the universe, but it was an important pimple to those whitefish. I called James that night. The next day we spent several hours observing them.

After 31 hours of observation over three weeks there were only two occasions when I saw whitefish leave the plume during the middle of the day. There was a clear reason. Whitefish are not as thermally tolerant as rainbow and cutthroat trout. But like most salmonids, they tend to grow best when temperatures are relatively stable and cool rather than shifting extremes. Each day the water temperature outside of the cool-seep was 63°F on morning arrival at 10 a.m., peaked at 74°F at 2 p.m. and eventually decreased to 68°F by dark. Whitefish try to avoid temperatures exceeding the lower- to mid-60s°F. The average water temperature where the seep entered the main river was 59°F, ranging from 57°F in the morning to 61°F during the middle of the day. Although their day-time foraging was limited to areas closest to the seep, the cooler temperatures and lesser variation meant the net energy loss for a fish with limited food resources was likely less than for a feeding fish that spent more energy roaming warmer temperatures outside the plume. Importantly, underwater lights revealed that the whitefish left the plume at dark to forage around the rest of the pool once water temperatures decreased. They were only trapped during the day.

The lush and dense riparian zone of an unlogged stream on the Oregon coast offers hope for future salmon populations.

Last man out leaves the lights on for the last time before deconstruction of the Glines Canyon Dam started the next morning.

The lower of the two dams – the Elwha Dam – being torn down, a process that is expected to take about two years.

The spawning activity of pink salmon is not only important for producing offspring, but their eggs and the insects they entrain during digging provide a critical food source to juveniles, such as the young steelhead in the front of the photo.

By the time the weather cooled four weeks later the whitefish school was down to eight individuals. Two had died or moved outside the two-mile reach, probably the former. The rest endured conditions unfavorable for survival through carefully orchestrated movements from a small cold-water base. I wondered if the whitefish would continue to use that relatively warm reach of river with its strategic cold-water plume in future summers. Unfortunately, two years later a flood buried the boulder in gravel. With the seep gone, whitefish no longer use that section of river. Regardless, I consider those whitefish as the equivalent of early nomads crossing Beringia, a straggling group inhabiting the edge of evolution's selective razor. Whether or not they survived, observing their attempt was an important lesson in how adaptation works. Their behavior was sufficiently compelling that James is now studying Calawah River whitefish for his graduate studies.

☙☙☙☙☙☙☙☙☙☙☙☙☙

The whitefish example is a microcosm of the salmon's struggle with rising water temperatures throughout the North Pacific Rim and provides reason for both optimism and pessimism. Other species are using similar tactics to mitigate short-term spikes in water temperature. For example, cold-water refuge areas are vital for rearing juvenile steelhead

Photograph by John McMillan for NOAA/NWFSC

Male pink salmon are better known as 'humpies' because of the protruding mound of cartilage on their backs. Here two males prepare to fight for access to a female pink in the Hunt Rd. side channel in the lower Elwha River.

The spawning salmon also provide food to other organisms, such as the raccoon and red-legged frogs. Therefore, removal of the Elwha dams will offer increasing benefits to these animals and others as salmon colonize the upper river and expand their distribution.

A juvenile steelhead only a few months in age pays closer attention to my camera than the sculpin below, which held still for several minutes until darting upwards and barely missing the naive fish. A lesson learned perhaps, or a sign of future shenanigans that will inevitably result in death. Nature will make the choice.

and Chinook in eastern Oregon streams where summer water temperatures commonly reach stressful and even lethal levels. Similarly, adult Chinook in the Yakima River basin have been documented using cool-water areas to decrease their body temperature and reduce energy expenditure as they fast through the summer until spawning. At a larger scale, summer steelhead migrating up the Columbia River rely heavily on the cool water at the mouths of colder tributaries.

This adaptable behavior is reason for optimism in a warming world. It allows salmon to survive for weeks to a few months in areas that would otherwise be uninhabitable. This is not necessarily because temperatures kill salmon outright, although that certainly happens, but more likely because chronic exposure to elevated temperatures heightens physiological stress reducing the immune response to disease, lowers fat stores that are important to spawning, and inhibits their ability to compete with expanding populations of more warm-water tolerant species for food and space. Ultimately, persistent increases in temperature will truncate salmonid distribution – especially cold-water dependent char species – but they have the ability to remain widely

There is no bird my father and I love more than the water ouzel. In our eyes they singularly epitomize a life's memories and experiences spent on rivers. The ouzel and their song is one of the wildlife constants throughout the year. In this photo a young ouzel is fat and happy with a protein-packed salmon egg, one of many it consumed while bobbing around behind several spawning coho salmon. Thanks to salmon, the ouzel remains beholden to streams through heat and rain, drought and flood: the bird of the river calendar.

distributed if adequate summer refugia are available. Nonetheless, the spatial template of the river calendar is certain to change.

While the whitefish revealed their adaptability in the face of drought, surviving long-term shifts in temperature and flow will require evolution in life history, not temporary behavioral tactics. The response of sockeye salmon to Columbia River temperature and flow changes related to agriculture and dams offers one example. Research by Dr. Tom Quinn and others at University of Washington found that since 1950 the timing of spring warming which determines shad and sockeye migration past Bonneville Dam has occurred increasingly earlier. Shad have kept up with the pace of this environmental change. The point at which 50% of the shad have migrated past Bonneville now occurs 38 days earlier than in 1938.

In contrast, sockeye have only increased their migration timing by five days, unable to keep up with warming's pace. It is critical that sockeye time upstream migration with cooler temperatures. Elevated temperatures will increase their metabolism, more quickly burning fat stores accumulated in the ocean. Without that fat they will not survive to spawn.

Summer steelhead and Chinook salmon are also shifting their run timing in relation to changes in Columbia River flow and temperature. Those fish that survive the changes will continue to alter their migration timing as their genetics allow, but the rate and extent of human-induced change in the interior Columbia will be too great for the adaptive abilities of some species, leaving behind a temporal void in the fabric of the river calendar.

Ultimately, changes in temperature and flow are only one problem: *habitat*. Salmon managers and scientists typically refer to four problems that are eerily analogous to the Four Horsemen of the Apocalypse, including hatcheries, hydropower, habitat and harvest. Climate change is now being considered a fifth "H": heat. My father and I see all of these problems as symptoms, rather than causes. Lives spent angling for, researching and observing salmon have revealed that there is only one H, that of *Homo sapiens*. We are the problem … or potentially the solution.

The human challenge is that of initiating solutions for sustainability. Rainbow trout isolated in the mountains of Mexico with retreat of the Ice Age some 15,000 years ago are proof that some wild salmonids, such as steelhead-turned-rainbow-trout, can survive dramatic warming. Some 10,000-50,000 years from now, during a future Ice Age, Mexican trout and other isolated populations may once again be linked to anadromy and the sea – a salmonid reawakening, or that of whatever fish evolves. But will that eventual reawakening include human life – or will other life forms fill our vacancy as an animal that for a time came to defy the selective pressures of nature?

Dad and I have no answers to the human questions. But we do understand that rivers represent our future – as necessary as the blood in our veins. And salmon provide the pulse of what we do to either protect rivers of the North Pacific Rim or to degrade them … for ourselves as well as for salmon. And like for Roderick Haig-Brown, we have come to understand ourselves through rivers ever awake with the movements of wild salmon and trout. We have come to love rivers, heart and soul, and we hope the photos stir something of what we have felt along North Pacific Rim rivers and what salmon, trout and char have taught us about their restless wakefulness that is ever-shifting nature. It is our song of thanks to Roderick Haig-Brown as one man who showed the way – an answering refrain to his song of rivers that don't sleep.

ᏉᏐᏉᏐᏉᏐᏉᏐᏉᏐᏉᏐᏉᏐᏉᏐᏉᏐ

While the river calendar will change, there are and will continue to be places of hope. Just as my father appropriately named his famed steelhead fly the "Winter's Hope" to convey a winter steelheader's emotional challenge, there are places that I have found while snorkeling that I believe epitomize the "salmon's hope." Each region of the Pacific Northwest still supports at least one river capable of supporting a great diversity and abundance of salmon. Even within the most challenging environments where salmon appear to have little chance at recovery, slices of their former heaven remain.

Many of the photographs that accompany this chapter were taken in the Elwha River where two dams have limited the anadromous salmon to the lower five miles of river since the early 1900s. Although salmon abundance and diversity has greatly declined, there is new reason for hope: the dams are being removed. I live on the Elwha River in James Starr's house, a little less than one mile above saltwater. Below the house, the river runs through a floodplain complex that is referred to as "Hunt Channel." The section of river is short, running only for 700 yards or so, but it is filled with big cottonwood, logjams and channel braids. It is one of the only places where suitable-sized spawning gravel remains, the supply in most of the lower river otherwise starved off by the dams.

In September of 2009 the Hunt Channel came alive with spawning pink and Chinook salmon. Hundreds of fish were stuffed into a short section of river and life responded. Underwater, juvenile salmon of all species and ages, sculpins, bull trout, frogs, salamanders and snakes gorged on salmon eggs.

*The haunting stare of a salmon carcass from bubbly
currents, sustaining life even in death.*

On bank, numerous bird and mammal species consumed the decaying carcasses. For a month, the abundance of spawning salmon created a biological Shangri-la in a river that is often thought to have gone asleep. The river calendar was momentarily as it should be on the Elwha in September, the life of salmon extending from the interstitial spaces of the river rocks where the sculpin live to the tops of the spruce trees where the eagles nest.

At night when it is quiet and I stand on the back porch, I hear only the Elwha. If I move to the other side of the house, I hear only the ocean's surf. There is a small point of calm between those two opposing sounds where I can hear both. It is a fleeting area and I must focus hard or one sound drowns out the other. Small places like the Hunt Channel are similar. It is easy to lose the beauty of special little places in the despair over larger regional losses. Further, they are often transient and finding them requires dedicated observation. Shangri-las exist though, probably in most watersheds to varying degrees. We humans must nurture these places and allow them to recover. Their fluttering pulse is the future of our salmon rivers.

To that end, we leave you with our personification of the wild-salmon's plea:

"Whether future heat or return of ice, just get out of our way.
We have long adapted to adversity."